THE BLACK KINGDOM OF THE NILE

The Nathan I. Huggins Lectures

The Black Kingdom of the Nile

CHARLES BONNET

With a Foreword by Henry Louis Gates, Jr.

HARVARD UNIVERSITY PRESS
Cambridge, Massachusetts
London, England
2019

Library of Congress Cataloging-in-Publication Data

Names: Bonnet, Charles, 1933– author. | Gates, Henry Louis, Jr., writer of foreword.

Title: The Black kingdom of the Nile / Charles Bonnet, with a foreword by
    Henry Louis Gates, Jr.

Description: Cambridge, Massachusetts : Harvard University Press, 2019. |
    Includes bibliographical references and index.

Identifiers: LCCN 2018040574 | ISBN 9780674986671 (hardcover : alk. paper)

Subjects: LCSH: Kerma (Extinct city) | Excavations (Archaeology)—Nubia. | Archaeology
    and history—Nile River Valley. | Nubia—Antiquities. | Nubia—History. | Nile River
    Valley—Antiquities.

Classification: LCC DT159.6.N83 B65 2019 | DDC 939/ .7801—dc23

LC record available at https://lccn.loc.gov/2018040574

Contents

PART 3 PNUBS DURING THE NEW KINGDOM, NAPATAN, AND MEROITIC PERIODS

Foreword

Over the past half century, Charles Bonnet's archaeological work in the Nile River Basin has rewritten the early history of the African continent and revolutionized our understanding of the interconnections between ancient Sudan and ancient Egypt. Most notably, his discoveries about the ancient civilization of Kerma, in present-day northern Sudan, refute the durable belief in the West that black African Nubian kingdoms were little more than Egyptian colonial outposts. This view had been strongly advanced in the first half of the twentieth century by Harvard professor of Egyptology George A. Reisner, whom all current archaeologists working in Sudan credit with naming and establishing Kerma as an important early African civilization from 2500 to 1500 BCE. However, Bonnet, unlike Reisner and other Egyptologists more generally, has always argued for Kerma's distinctly indigenous culture, which peaked between 1785 and 1500 BCE, when it was the capital of the kingdom of Kush. Bonnet's literally groundbreaking work has shown that, far from being a colony of Egypt, Kerma was a powerful southern *rival*. It was the center of a complex, prosperous society that was independent of its northern neighbor and maintained its own culture, methods of construction, and burial customs.

Although Egypt seized Kerma and conquered the Kingdom of Kush around 1500 BCE, Bonnet's work also examines the powerful kingdom that emerged in the same region seven centuries later, whose leaders would become known as the "Black Pharaohs" of Egypt's Twenty-Fifth Dynasty (ca. 744–656 BCE). In 2003, near Kerma, Bonnet unearthed an astounding find: seven well-preserved and largely intact monumental stone statues. These statues portray five of these pharaohs (two in double image), the first of whom ruled over Nubia, Egypt, and Palestine for more than a quarter century: Taharqa, Tanutamun, Senkamanisken, Anlamani, and Aspelta. Bonnet studied these statues, restored them, and built a museum for them—with a Sudanese architect and using his own funds—at Kerma. Any scholar researching the economy, culture, and exercise of power in early African civilizations owes a tremendous debt to Charles Bonnet and his lifelong labors.

Bonnet's excavations essentially rewrote the early history of civilization on the African continent.

Beginning in the late 1970s, he unearthed evidence of a well-defended, densely populated urban settlement at the heart of an agriculturally fertile region. Home to a thriving culture, Kerma was also enriched by its trade in gold, ivory, ebony, and cattle and by its location at the crossroads of desert routes linking Egypt, the Red Sea, and the kingdoms of sub-Saharan Africa. We now know more not only about everyday life but also about the everyday rituals of death in the ancient world as a result of Bonnet's exploration of Kerma's extensive necropolis, which has revealed the contents of thousands of tombs. Bonnet's later explorations at Dukki Gel, one kilometer north of Kerma, shed light on a major Nubian city of the mid-second millennium BCE, revealing evidence of the erosion of a distinct Kerma culture following the Egyptian occupation under Thutmose I in the early fifteenth century BCE, while his discovery of the statues of the Black Pharaohs of the Twenty-Fifth Dynasty shows the revival of a powerful black Nubian society and culture seven hundred years later.

In addition to his scholarly discoveries, Bonnet has been praised for his strong relationship with Sudanese historians and government officials and for ensuring that the local population has been involved in all of his projects. He continues to act as an ambassador for Nubia to the Nubian diaspora around the world. This ambassadorial quality was on full view during the Nathan I. Huggins Lectures on which this book is based. The audience comprised many of the Harvard community's "usual suspects," but in addition, each day we saw dozens of Nubians from Boston and New York—scholars, families, and admirers of the man whom they rightly saw as restoring Nubia to the historical record with both accuracy and dignity. *The Black Kingdom of the Nile* is the first book of Bonnet's to be published initially in English (much of his work is available in translation, of course). That Harvard University Press is publishing this book is a fitting tribute to Bonnet's long career and to the long history of Harvard scholarship on Nubia and Nubia's relation to Egypt.

For the entirety of their oral and written history in the United States, African Americans have been fascinated by Nubia and its environs as the seat of pre-European, pre-transatlantic slave trade power. When

African Americans say, "We come from kings and queens," it is the idea of Nubia to which they refer. When multiple hair care companies use "Nubian" in their names, they do so to invoke a beautiful, powerful, and intact royal blackness. When W. E. B. Du Bois, who earned his Ph.D. in history at Harvard in 1895—ten years before George Reisner joined the university's faculty—wished to invoke the origins of "Negro genius," he located its roots in "the valley of the Nile from Meroe and Nepata down to the great temples of Egypt."

The terms "Kush," "Cushites," "Meroe," "Ethiopians," and "Nubians" have all been used, with varying degrees of both accuracy and mythologizing, as signifiers for the place and the people of the region that the work of Bonnet and others has shown to be a realm of architectural, economic, and cultural cosmopolitanism and sophistication. If the early kingdom of Kush, centered at Kerma, emerged in Nubia toward the end of the third millennium BCE, a revived kingdom of Kush reappeared in the early eighth century BCE, with its first capital at Napata. Having conquered Egypt about 720 BCE, the Black Pharaohs made their capital in Egypt at Memphis. When the Assyrians invaded Egypt during the 660s BCE, the royal court retreated to Napata, bringing the Twenty-Fifth Dynasty to a close; eventually it moved further south to Meroe, which became the capital of Kush for the next thousand years. Known for metallurgy, its still untranslated written script, its pottery, and its hybrid culture, it was also known for having several powerful queens, the *kandake,* who have given rise to the trope of the Nubian queen in African and African American culture. (The *kandake* is familiar from the New Testament: Acts 8:26–40 recounts the conversion narrative of "an Ethiopian, a eunuch, a court official of Candace, the queen of the Ethiopians," and the familiar woman's name Candace is indeed derived from these African roots.)

Especially in the nineteenth century, African American authors looked to the kingdoms of Kush, Nubia, and ancient Ethiopia as key to understanding their cultural antecedents. The recounting of this history of sovereignty and power provided a decisive counternarrative to slavery and its concomitant debasement of Africans and their descendants and also gave deep context to these authors' own claims to the right to possess learning, culture, and civilization. In addition to Du Bois, authors including Prince Hall, James Pennington, Robert Benjamin Lewis, Edward Wilmot Blyden, William Wells Brown, Martin R. Delany, George Washington Williams, Rufus Perry, Leila Amos Pendleton, and Drusilla Houston all evoked and reimagined Nubia in their attempts to refute racist claims about the subhuman nature of Africans and their lack of a history of "civilization."

It is this region so cherished in the African and the African American imagination that Charles Bonnet has realized for us through his prodigious archaeological efforts. His work has also drawn more researchers to this region, which had once been essentially forgotten; there are now more than forty international archaeological teams working in collaboration with Sudanese archaeologists.

Perhaps Bonnet's most dramatic contribution to the early history of Africa—even more dramatic than the unearthing of the magnificent statues of the Black Pharaohs—was in Kerma, Sudan, where his team has exposed an early fortified, complex, and sophisticated royal city with palaces, temples, workshops, residences, and a huge ceremonial center in a suburb about one kilometer north, known as Dukki Gel. Timothy Kendall, who along with Bonnet is one of the leading archaeologists of ancient Nubia and current-day Sudan, told me the following about Dukki Gel in an email exchange:

[In Dukki Gel] Bonnet has found a series of gigantic, complex mudbrick structures, without architectural parallel except in central Africa, showing a preference for curvilinear ground plans, going back many centuries. Following the Egyptian conquest, these structures were overbuilt by a large Egyptian precinct with rectilinear temples and palaces. Oddly, throughout the era of Egyptian occupation, small round temples continued to exist beside the Egyptian temples, suggesting an Egyptian tolerance for the native cults—or perhaps a merging of native Kushite gods with Egyptian gods. The archaeological patterns suggest the presence of two or more different population groups, coexisting side by side for centuries.

Bonnet's labors have shown that sub-Saharan and Nilotic cultures existed in tandem, in mutual dependence, and with complex interactions of power. His insistence on this coexistence, backed by archaeological findings and architectural facts, is precisely what has made Charles Bonnet's work so transformative.

Charles Bonnet was born into a wine-growing family near Geneva, Switzerland, in 1933, and at age twenty-two earned a diploma at the Marcelin / Morges School of Agriculture near Lausanne. He credits his early exposure to viniculture with some responsibility for his subsequent career in archaeology. In a 2010 interview, he said, "One learns how to see the ground, the vegetation, the colours of the ground." In 1965, after graduating from the School of Oriental Studies in Geneva, he made his first archaeological visit to Sudan. He recalled that at the time he was told, "You are wasting your time; there is nothing in Sudan." No one says that anymore, largely owing to Bonnet's excavations and scholarship (more than 150 articles and books) over the past fifty years.

In terms of Harvard's history in African studies, Charles Bonnet has decisively extended and revised the early work of Harvard's premier Egyptologist, George Reisner. In terms of African history and world history, he has added to the archaeological record in illuminating, necessary, and field-shaping ways. It was a distinct honor to welcome Professor Bonnet to Harvard University in October 2016 to host his exciting and exceptionally well-received Nathan I. Huggins Lectures in African and African American History, "The Double Capital of Kush: Kerma and Dukki Gel," that gave rise to this important new volume.

I would like to thank Tim Kendall, Rita Freed, Abby Wolf, and Amy Alemu for their invaluable contributions to my foreword.

Henry Louis Gates, Jr.
Alphonse Fletcher University Professor
Harvard University

THE BLACK KINGDOM OF THE NILE

Introduction

From November to February the extreme climate of northern Sudan is at its most pleasant for the visitor and thus most suitable for archaeological exploration. An often violent north wind can, however, reverse these favorable conditions, stripping the soil or, alternatively, covering the most meticulously cleared surface with dust. This powdery Nile silt has enriched the soil and furthered the development of agriculture since Neolithic times, creating conditions ideal for human habitation. In both Egypt and Nubia, complex cultures arose along the riverbank thanks to annual flooding and extensive irrigation. It is therefore hardly surprising to find in this region the vestiges of the first African kingdoms, dating back five millennia and more. For many years research was concentrated in the north, adjacent to the cultural centers of the Near East and the Mediterranean basin. Central Africa remained outside the sphere of large-scale archaeological excavation.

Beginning in the Old Kingdom Egyptian pharaohs attempted to conquer these remote regions and gain control of the routes to gold, ivory, ebony, and exotic animals (Roccati 1982). But conquest was difficult, as evidenced by the construction of a defensive line at the Second Cataract by the Sesostris pharaohs, masters of the art of war and most distrustful of local forces to the south and in the Eastern and Western Deserts (Trigger 1976, 64–81). The Egyptians encountered formidable populations that also appeared to benefit from a warrior tradition, to this day little studied. Many confrontations characterized these older periods, but it was not until the beginning of the New Kingdom that the conflicts intensified.

Archaeological data have supplemented Egyptian sources, opening up new perspectives and allowing us to elaborate what amounts to a counterhistory of the Nile Valley, partially based on past research. Our approach will certainly need time to be verified. It is especially necessary to investigate the sites of central Sudan to better understand the points of contact in the network that supported increasing centralization by the Kerma kings. The numerous seals and impressions recovered in the city attest to its control of trade, which must have contributed greatly to the development of the kingdom. So did its geographic location: north of the Sahel, situated between Egypt, sub-Saharan Africa, and the Red

Fig. 1   General view of the Western Deffufa

Sea. The first stage of our work, comprising several seasons of excavation, led us to the conclusion that the monument dominating the site, known as the Deffufa (Fig. 1), was actually the principal temple of the city (Bonnet and Valbelle 2004). George Reisner, influenced by the discovery of a very large number of objects from Egypt, identified the Deffufa as the palace of an Egyptian governor. This conclusion, while called into question some twenty years later, hardly detracts from the remarkable work that this genius of Egyptology conducted at the site for several years, or from his publications, still most useful to this day (Reisner 1923a, 1923b). With no texts to back us up—Kerma was not a literate culture—our own interpretation has not received immediate acceptance. Verification will require further evidence from continuing research in Nubia,

and synthesizing the mass of scientific data will be the work of decades.

During the second major stage of our expedition, we realized that the city, which we have been able to clear in its entirety over a period of thirty years, was the capital of an independent kingdom (Fig. 2). Urbanization began circa 2400 BCE and led very rapidly to the emergence of a complex state, partially inspired by the example of Egypt (Bonnet and Valbelle 2014). The presence of numerous institutions, large secular and religious structures, and spacious dwellings in strategic locations reflects the centralization of power and indicates a hierarchical society in control of the exchange of goods. More complicated still was the study of military defenses constructed mainly of wood and *galous,* a mix of silt, straw, and dung shaped into large clods.

KERMA NORTH,
TUMBUS

1. Capital of the Kingdom of Kerma
2. Site Museum and Kerma Center
3. Port Quarter, Temple, Royal Tomb
4. Indigenous ceremonial City of Dokki Gel
5. Napatan Neighborhood
6. Western Cemeteries
7. Eastern Necropolis

BURGEIG, ARGO ►

0   500   1000 m

Fig. 2   Topographical plan of the archaeological sites of Kerma

The third stage of our investigations is relatively recent, no more than eight years old. It includes the discovery of the ceremonial city of Dukki Gel, 700 meters north of the Nubian capital (Bonnet 2013, 807–823). Excavation and geomagnetic survey have exposed an architectural style more African than Egyptian in character, associated perhaps with populations originating in central Sudan, where kingdoms had already attained a high level of development. Admittedly, we know almost nothing about this region, so remote from Kerma, and we can only hope that contemporaneous discoveries in Darfur, Kordofan, Kassala, and the land of Punt will one day complete the picture.

After fifty long years of excavation lasting three months per season, it is time for a report. We began at the site of Tabo. Clearing the temple of the Nubian pharaoh Taharqa produced impressive remains of the Twenty-Fifth Dynasty (Bonnet 2011a, 283–293), when Nubian kings ruled over both Egypt and Nubia. The hospitality of neighbors adjoining the archaeological site greatly helped our expedition, especially since there were no modern means of communication. Crossing the desert between Khartoum and Dongola was even more difficult, as seasonal rains sculpted the trails into fearsome relief. The hours we spent perched on bundles of supplies in the beds of overheated trucks, often buffeted by the wind, largely inured us to discomfort, which in any case was quickly forgotten upon encountering the generosity of the people we met during our adventures. We had lessons in patience: learning to wait was the order of the day. Colleagues who followed one after the other during the years of excavation, as well as Sudanese workers—several of whom collaborated faithfully for five decades—contributed immeasurably to the success of our mission. Workers from several villages grew skilled at cleaning mudbrick masonry and highlighting specific details, as well as tracing the impressions left behind by wood. This extended apprenticeship has been a guarantee of our success, and we certainly hope that it will continue.

PART I

Kerma, Capital of Nubia

History of the Expedition

Lengthy archaeological research conducted at the famous site of Kerma familiarized us with its poorly preserved remains, the exception being the Western Deffufa. Its distinctive outline had been mentioned by all former visitors, who associated it with a second monument, the Eastern Deffufa, visible on the horizon 4 kilometers to the east (Bonnet and Valbelle 2000, 112–134). The Nubian term *deffufa* denotes a massive man-made structure. George Reisner conducted salvage excavations at Kerma before the introduction of an extensive farming program in the fertile soils of the plain. At the beginning of our expedition, it was still possible to see the enormous steam engine, now abandoned, that operated the pumps. The Egyptologist wished to safeguard the entire site but was soon forced to admit that the archaeological remains were too extensive; excavation had to be more selective. Thus, after clearing the Western Deffufa and its quarter, he determined that the remains surrounding it were less significant, so he concentrated instead on the necropolis, one of the most impressive of the ancient world.

During our first seasons, we considered the interpretation of the Deffufas, still a matter of controversy, to be one of our first priorities, while at the same time beginning the rescue of neighboring sites endangered by the spread of the modern city as well as cultivation. For these two major monuments, it seemed most likely that the techniques developed for the archaeology of structures would provide some answers, as it did in the analysis of medieval European buildings. Indeed, examining the elevations of the Western Deffufa allowed us to identify fourteen phases of masonry (Fig. 3). It soon became evident that the building had been modified continuously and its evolution could be verified only with thorough stratigraphic study. We discovered that the earlier levels were even more numerous: forty of these have been identified. Elsewhere, foundation deposits beneath an enclosure wall and the masonry of a chapel attested to the religious function of the site. The Western Deffufa was thus the principal temple of the city for more than a thousand years (Bonnet 1978, 113–116; 1980, 43–50; 2014).

To establish as exact a chronology as possible, it was necessary to follow the classification of Kerma cultures proposed by Brigitte Gratien: Early Kerma from 2400

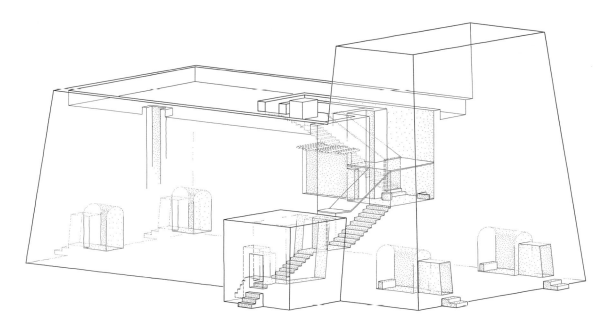

Fig. 3 Axonometric reconstruction of the Western Deffufa during Classic Kerma

to 2050 BCE, Middle Kerma from 2050 to 1750 BCE, and Classic Kerma from 1750 to 1450 BCE. Final Kerma corresponds to the end of the kingdom with the conquests by the Thutmosids in the early New Kingdom (Gratien 1978). It was thus decided to excavate several sectors of the eastern necropolis. Tomb typology would produce a topographical chronology that, together with the development of funerary customs and the seriation of archaeological material, would increase the accuracy of dating. Twenty-four sectors with ten to twenty tombs each yielded rich finds, notably imported ceramics from Egypt that provided extensive comparative material (Privati 1998; 1999; Bourriau 1998). More recently, Matthieu Honegger undertook the excavation of several hundred Early Kerma tombs and discovered that these burials had begun even earlier, in approximately 2550 BCE. Radiocarbon analysis and the abundance of pottery have contributed to this precision.

Having established a solid stratigraphic sequence in the religious quarter in the center of the city (Bonnet and Valbelle 2004, 74–95), we attempted to correlate known layers with remains spread over more than 25 hectares. Since systematic in-depth excavation was not feasible, we chose instead to conduct extensive surface clearing to produce a horizontal stratigraphy. We quickly discovered that almost the entire area had served as a cemetery during the Napatan and Meroitic periods, damaging earlier remains. Besides tomb monuments, the ground was riddled with ditches and long, sloping passages leading to funerary chambers. Surface clearing became the favored method for establishing the plan of the city, while sondages were more practical for retrieving ceramic evidence for the refinement of the chronology.

These excavation methods also took into consideration how the site would appear after the excavation work was finished. The erosion of mudbrick structures was, in places, 0.30 to 0.50 meters deep. It was not unusual for several sweeps of the brush to reveal two or three periods of construction. Since foundations, once uncovered, can rapidly disappear in strong winds, they must be protected. Using ancient methods, great quantities of mudbrick were manufactured in varying dimensions, and walls

Fig. 4 Aerial view of the ancient city of Kerma after restoration

were covered with two, three, or four courses of brick, depending on the state of conservation of the building in question (Fig. 4). The foundations thus protected clearly reveal building plans, and the view from the top of the Deffufa shows off the urban area to best advantage. Since ancient cityscapes are extremely rare in the Nile Valley, this Nubian example is especially welcome.

As many as seventy workers were divided into teams of fifteen to twenty—basket carriers and more specialized workers—under the direction of *raïs*. Most of the workers were quite experienced, having worked at Tabo and the Western Necropolis of Kerma. The *raïs* were trained during several European visits. The principal supervisors came from the farming community, while Bedouin families settled in the area for three or four generations also contributed to our work. Scrapers, adzes, and brushes were

the best tools for extensive surface clearing; the quality of the final cleaning has led to the understanding of the structures preserved. This meticulous cleaning also allowed us to plot, on a large scale, all the cleared brickwork. The extensive plan drawn to a scale of 1:20 has greatly aided reconstruction. This plan, including scale reductions, was produced several decades ago with photographic techniques no longer in use today.

This extensive clearing took place during some thirty seasons, conducted at the same time as salvage excavations in the modern city. Once we determined that activity next to the principal site was threatening the ancient city, we resolved to build a protective wall of *galous* more than 2 meters high, replacing our original fence of metal stakes and barbed wire, which had to be dismantled every year. This new wall, still in existence, has been most

Fig. 5   Kerma site museum

effective. We also decided to conduct an excavation along the west side of the necropolis. Trucks and other utility vehicles passing the tumulus were causing continuous destruction, especially to surface deposits. Recent work in the area has also included long-term protection of this unique funerary ensemble.

All these activities have led to encounters with local inhabitants, and guided tours have been organized for both adults and schoolchildren. The building of a museum in 2008 (Fig. 5) is also raising awareness of their patrimony among the local Sudanese. Constructed next to the Western Deffufa, the museum includes a general presentation of excavation results from all expedition sites. The main attraction for visitors is seven monumental statues of stone, discovered in a cache at the site of Dukki Gel, where we were obliged to conduct an unscheduled excavation because there, too, the expansion of agricultural fields and palm groves threatened important remains. In order to protect what would become, to

researchers, the ancient city of Pnubs, we built a high wall insulating the site. The work begun there almost twenty years ago continues: after clearing the temples of the Nubian empires of Napata and Meroe, we focused on the buildings belonging to the New Kingdom Egyptian conquest, including several temples and palaces of the great pharaohs of the Eighteenth Dynasty. Then we had to conduct an in-depth excavation of a Nubian settlement; and just recently, we conducted a salvage excavation at the exterior of the protective wall, in a palm grove that was being converted to farmland. There we discovered an extension of the indigenous city with several monumental gates. We found ourselves at the origins of Sudanese history and hope that it will be possible to preserve this part of the past. The adventure of archaeology is ever present in our lengthy Nubian undertaking and has yielded discoveries that have enriched our understanding of relations with the center of the African continent.

The Fortress at the Beginning of Early Kerma

The first settlement was founded at Kerma between 2500 and 2400 BCE (Bonnet and Valbelle 2014, 216–228). At this time the inhabitants moved closer to the main course of the Nile due to progressive warming, which resulted in the drying up of the river branches in the plain. This gradual desertification required farming and herding populations to alter their way of life. The necropolis associated with the settlement was established 4 kilometers to the east, next to a branch of the Nile also in the process of desiccation. In the 1960s the remains of several pottery workshops were identified next to the southwest burial area. Most likely their output was destined for funeral rites that included sharing a meal with the deceased, after which mourners upended the food bowls and left them on the surface, along the edge of the tumulus. The kiln type in these workshops is characteristic of Early Kerma. The urban center developed on an island that itself expanded in length. The contours of the island were most likely determined by large bends in the river; the inhabitants of the city may have dug ditches in order to correct its course. From earliest times legumes and grain were planted along the sides of ditches once flood waters receded. Traces of a wooden plowshare in the loose soil as well as holes for the planting of seeds were still visible in places, as if planting had been interrupted and the plot abandoned to the sun. Other traces were found in the ditches, including human footprints and bovine hoofprints in front of entryways.

From the very beginning a north-south route was established, probably leading to the site of Dukki Gel to the north and, 1 kilometer to the south, to the riverbank, where the first port may already have been founded (Fig. 6). This thoroughfare was faced with earthwork bastions reinforced with wooden posts. One of these bastions projected slightly, its wall 1.20 to 2.30 meters thick and forming a prominent U-shape 10 meters long and 3 meters wide. Elsewhere, postholes and other remains led to the reconstruction of additional installations that may have served to isolate the road from surrounding construction work. The remains of a square fortress 80 meters to a side were located to the east. Thousands of later postholes complicated interpretation, but several earthworks, whitish in color, made it possible to trace an enclosure wall to the south. It

Fig. 6   Plan of the Early Kerma city

was no more than 2 meters thick, supported by connected bastions 15 to 16 meters in length. A gateway opening onto the north-south road was flanked by two smaller bastions, identified by their many postholes. On the north side of the settlement, the remains of a sandy beach probably indicated the bank of a Nile meander. Stratigraphy northeast of the Deffufa reached the underlying natural layer. The first occupation levels included a group of small circular buildings 3 meters in diameter, clearly distinguishable from later such structures, which generally measured around 4.3 meters. Discarded animal bones were found along their perimeter, most often on the south side. A cult installation was probably established in the center of the fortified city, in the inaccessible layers under the Deffufa. To the west of the Deffufa we found long wooden buildings 3.5 to 4 meters in width by approximately 10 meters in length, dimen-

sions that facilitated the construction of a relatively short-beamed roof. Judging by the succession of postholes, this area of rectangular buildings was long-lived. The buildings may have served as annexes to the cult installation, which we assume was located beneath the Deffufa. We have not exposed the entirety of this complex in order to avoid destroying levels destined for future analysis. Likewise, we did not undertake a systematic survey of all the traces of wooden structures because it would have significantly complicated and slowed down our research, but we have taken them into consideration. Demographic interpretations are therefore based on poorly conserved and insubstantial architecture that yielded incomplete information. The fortress from the beginnings of Early Kerma testifies to the emergence of a strong power at the origins of the first kingdom.

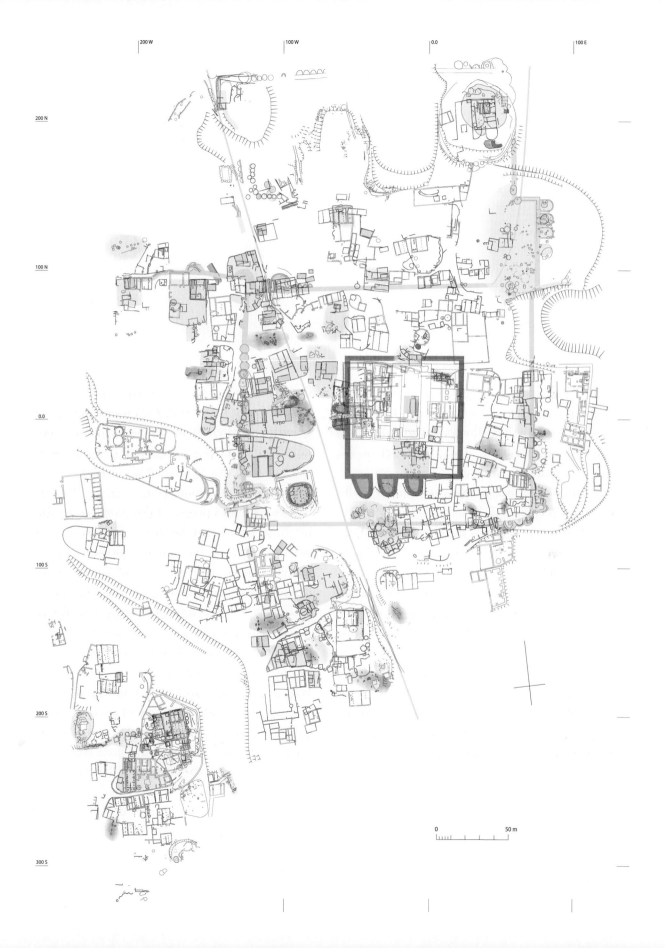

200 W
100 W
0.0
100 E

200 N

100 N

0.0

100 S

200 S

300 S

0   50 m

The Early Kerma City

It is also during the Early Kerma period that an ambitious program of urbanization took place (Fig. 6). A new wall enclosed a city of noteworthy proportions, measuring 200 by 170 meters. The plan followed an existing organization, with gateways located in accordance with earlier traffic patterns (Bonnet and Valbelle 2014, 219–224). Clearly the north-south roadway remained the principal route, and several thoroughfares were developed perpendicular to it. While the fortified city played a central role, other concentrations existed outside the walls: to the north, a temple was surrounded by several annexes and a defensive system; to the southwest, a religious installation was established in a secondary urban complex, on the other side of a wide ditch. Traces of fortified walls toward the north and west indicate expansion over neighboring areas, where the potters' workshops were once located. The quadrangle wall exhibited several types of defenses, doubtless corresponding to different phases of construction through the centuries. Our results are limited and remain to be confirmed, as the remains of the wall and its bastions, generally constructed of *galous*

on alluvial levels, were largely destroyed by later structures; nor has wind erosion spared some of the foundations. Extensive postholes related to the fortifications indicate that these mixed structures of *galous* and wood were fairly complex, making their interpretation quite problematic.

This system of placing the bastions alongside a rectilinear wall existed throughout Early Kerma. The bastions were constructed using large posts along the length of the northeast wall of the quadrangular enclosure, sometimes anchored in circular masonry sunk more or less deeply into the ground. Another system consisted of a series of massive circular structures 6 meters in diameter, connected to one another by short rectilinear segments. This construction method was used for the western enclosure wall, which presented an undulating surface of considerable height. This technique can be found in some fortifications erected after the Egyptian conquest.

The bastions attached to the southeast corner of the quadrangular enclosure were constructed in courses of *galous* 0.40 meters thick, the courses increasingly set back to produce a slope. Entry was through a doorway into a rounded inner room.

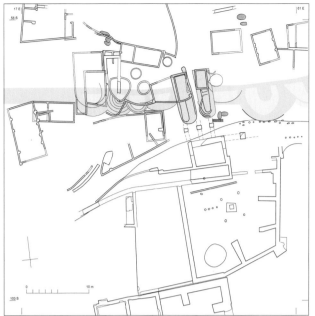

Fig. 7 Gates of Early Kerma and Middle Kerma

Stakes helped consolidate the structure; their general shape is slightly pointed or pear-shaped. On the eastern side, in contrast, the *galous* bastions, 3 meters in length, were separated from each other by intervals of approximately 4 meters. Near the southeast gate, where the enclosure wall was subsequently enlarged, it is characterized by small towers 3 meters in diameter anchored in circular foundations. Spaced bastions supporting a rectilinear wall were frequent in Egyptian fortifications, notably in the city of Kor near Buhen. At Kerma, however, the system of placing bastions side by side or connecting them with a rectilinear wall was more common.

The gates were generally flanked by twin parallel bastions aligned longitudinally (Fig. 7), a plan also recognized at Kor. At Kerma the bastions had narrow rooms, intended for the guards, on their inner sides; the ramps of a lateral stairway provided access to the tops of the bastions. The doorways were very narrow: 0.70 meters wide, just enough for a man and a laden donkey to pass through. On the west side two gates stood out clearly from the others. The simplest one formed a long, narrow corridor leading to the urban core. This gate was flanked on the north by large circular structures alternating with rectangular rooms; on the south by a projecting tripartite structure possibly supporting guardrooms above (Fig. 8). The second entry was more monumental in nature; access was by means of a long sunken lane rising to a level 2 or 3 meters higher in the city itself (Fig. 9). A wooden gate was built at the end of a narrow, twisting passage with tower-like structures on either side. They were constructed of circles of sunken piles, in front of which a fence of posts delimited a series of platforms. On the inside of the gate, the passageway narrowed to a width of 0.70 meters because of a large quadrangular structure consisting of closely spaced posts. Barriers were also noted along the interior passage. This principal gateway led to a sector of the city occupied by large royal buildings. The wood-and-earth construction of the gate reflects the Nubian tradition. Doubtless other fortifications existed nearby, but later constructions have obliterated platform foundations that must once have stretched for 20 meters. A series of warehouses and cattle enclosures was located not far from the

Fig. 8   Western gates of Early Kerma and Middle Kerma

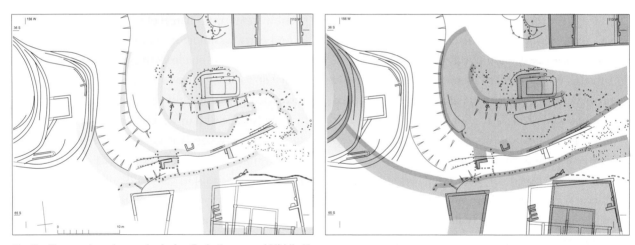

Fig. 9   The great western gate during Early Kerma and Middle Kerma

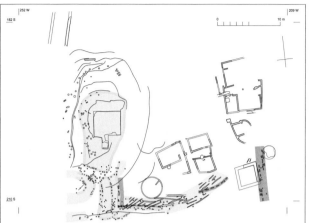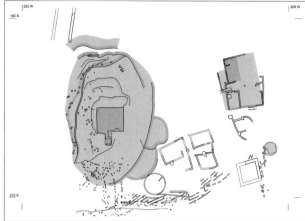

Fig. 10   Western gates of the secondary urban complex during Early Kerma and Middle Kerma

opening of the gate. Thousands of hoofprints are evidence that livestock was herded inside the fortifications when the city was under attack. The varying diameters of the stakes and posts used to construct the enclosure were associated with several Early Kerma building periods. This city gate remained in use until the end of the kingdom of Kerma.

There existed another gateway during this early period, located to the west of the secondary urban complex and destined to become the seat of a most important religious establishment (Fig. 10). The corners of several barriers, a fence 1.50 meters thick, and other structural remains indicate very early occupation at this site, perhaps even before the arrival of the Egyptian expeditions of the Old Kingdom Sixth Dynasty. During a second phase, but still in Early Kerma, the western hillslopes and the gateway were completely transformed, a complex fortified entry replacing its much simpler predecessor. A passage protected by barriers rounded the foot of the hill. The gate, located on the hillslope, led to a defensive platform in the middle of the hill and to a ramp up to a plateau. Rows of postholes have been found on the escarpment between the hill and the

plateau. Wooden structures fortified the break in the slope, while next to the religious precinct bastions completed the defensive system. On the other side, dominating the ditch to the northeast, a wall flanked by small bastions (2 meters by 1 meter) protected a building with two wings placed at right angles to each other. The original mudbrick building must already have served a religious function. It seems clear that this location served a religious function from earliest days: chapels constructed of posts, founded during the Early Kerma period, were rebuilt several times on the same consecrated ground. The oldest such structures averaged about 4 meters in diameter.

In the city the north-south road, oriented at an angle to the quadrangle enclosure, served to align the major monuments. The road was continuously protected by a renovated defensive system in the center of the city as well as at either end. The religious precinct was enlarged and wooden annexes rebuilt on an elongated plan. Other buildings were constructed of mudbrick. Evidence from the single trial trench excavated in the center of the Deffufa would seem to indicate the existence of a large cult structure also of mudbrick. Dwellings spread along

the south side of the building that would become
the major temple. Also of mudbrick, they were constructed on top of numerous grain storage pits belonging to an area of round structures associated with
the first fortress. Ceramic material dates these levels of
occupation between 2500 and 2400 BCE. The houses
consisted of a single room, sometimes with a gated
courtyard containing aboveground circular silos with
thin walls. In Egypt, contemporary houses of this type
have been found at both Aswan and Giza.

Two residential complexes were located opposite
the principal religious precinct. The southern complex was enclosed by a serpentine wall ending in a
semicircle along the north-south axis road; this wall
underwent several phases of restoration. A potter's
workshop was found in this area; the pit kilns, filled
with ash, may be very old, but their chronology is
uncertain since they were used to fire crude ceramics
that are difficult to date. The main residence of the
Early Kerma period is the largest that we have discovered in the city, measuring 14.80 by 13.50 meters. Its plan of two independent building complexes
separated by a central courtyard is typically Nubian.
The fairly thin walls, just 0.20 meters thick, were

generally supported by pilasters of equal width. The
building in the eastern complex, accessible through
the interior courtyard, was divided into two rooms
with a doorway in between. The second complex,
almost identical in size to the southern complex, included two units. The first consisted of two buildings with an interior central courtyard; the second
contained two contiguous buildings served by a
courtyard. The remains of a kitchen were observed
opposite the first of these houses and a water storage
area against the façade of the second. These twin residences, strategically located between two city gates,
may be interpreted as royal in nature (Fig. 6). They
are similar in character to the residences of the sul-
tans of Darfur toward the end of the Middle Ages.

As we have seen, the stretch of north-south road
in front of the entrance to the central temple was
protected by an enormous bastion dating to the first
period of settlement. The remains of several military
constructions of silt and wooden stakes led us to
conclude that the gate to a temenos was equally well
fortified. On the other side of the main axis, we uncovered a bastion that had replaced a previous
construction. This new defense, 18 to 20 meters in

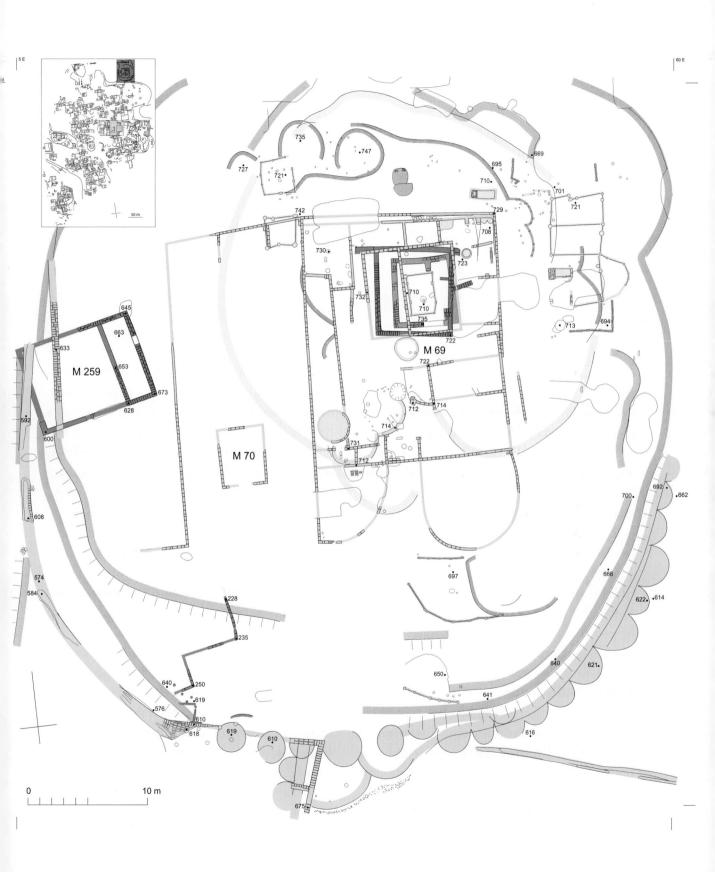

diameter, included a military barracks in its center reinforced with brick masonry. This massive structure defending the axis road was part of a truly impressive complex of fortifications.

In the direction of Dukki Gel to the northeast we discovered a vast cult complex, founded perhaps during the first settlement of the city; all that remained were a few segments of a circular temenos wall. The area thus defined formed a circle 30 meters in diameter; postholes delimited a small building 3 meters by 2 meters in the center (Fig. 11). Several cult installations were built and rebuilt in this location. The entrance to the temenos was defined by two bastions. On the eastern side two large wooden buildings and an enclosed courtyard belonged to temple administration. Other square buildings and a circular silo were located next to the primitive chapel which, however, soon developed the characteristics of a temple. It is interesting to note that a processional way connected the entrance of this cult installation to the rear of the principal temple in the city; it is possible that this processional road continued all the way to the city of Dukki Gel. Traces of construction around the cult site consisted of large postholes, but there is no doubt that the walls were of *galous*. The posts served simply as support.

Urbanization extended to the outskirts of the quadrangular city, where several mudbrick dwellings were discovered. Their plans, irregular in nature, probably indicate social differences. They range from small single-roomed dwellings to residences of two or three separate buildings with internal courtyards and spacious exteriors that included circular silos for food storage and enclosures for small livestock. Along a northeastern extension of the eastern wall of the city, an in-depth study of Early Kerma levels was possible. Several round structures were excavated, along with grain pits dug into the alluvial soil. Winding palisades defined different properties. One of these structures stands out in particular, with its hearth inside a double circle of posts. Measuring up to 5.50 meters in diameter, these structures were larger than the ones discovered in great quantity inside and around the city. This area also contained a small cemetery, where we excavated several tombs. These burials belonged to modest individuals and were devoid of grave goods except for one or two pots and a few beads. The bodies were interred in a flexed or contracted position, often on their right side with the head to the east, as was common during the Kerma periods.

Along the west wall of the original fortress, which was leveled in antiquity, we noted several hundred postholes that must have belonged to wooden constructions. The ground had been compacted to provide a foundation for a group of structures. The central building was remarkable for the care taken in its construction and by a square room approximately 8 meters to a side, an exceptional size for this period. The room was flanked on the west by a rectangular complex and on the south by what appears to be a trapezoidal vestibule. The presence of associated buildings, and especially of a pathway leading to the south, has led us to interpret this complex as the first ceremonial palace dating to the end of Early Kerma. During Middle Kerma, a ceremonial way was established west of the religious precinct. Thus we have a first palace, followed by a second one outside the temenos.

The city with its quadrangular enclosure defines a major stage of urbanization. While construction in wood and *galous* was still common, the use of mudbrick was becoming the norm for religious and royal buildings, as well as for the residences of the more prominent citizenry and for some military installations. For the enclosure wall itself and its bastions, however, the traditional *galous* technique remained in use, specifically in elongated structures built in courses 0.40 meters high. As at the southern end of the religious precinct, we can conclude that most houses were in the form of circular wooden structures. Our picture of the Early Kerma city is thus incomplete, especially for the outlying districts. It is possible to imagine that when the Egyptian expeditions of the Sixth Dynasty reached Kerma, the kingdom was already well established, with organized institutions, a strong army, and a centralized royal power.

The Middle Kerma City

During the centuries of the Middle Kerma period, urbanization was complete (Fig. 12) (Bonnet and Valbelle 2014, 224–229). Houses were increasingly spacious, opening onto an exterior courtyard; they appear to have belonged to an upper class with greater means. Religious institutions increased their holdings and undertook ambitious municipal building programs. In the secondary urban complex, chapels were more numerous and several were rebuilt on a grander scale, with workshops for the preparation of offerings. Clusters of ovens supplied the numerous cult installations. Once again the general topography of the site was modified to take into account the bends of the Nile. Major works changed the city limits, and ditches were dug into the center. On all four sides of the city, areas were left free of construction for defensive purposes; this layout evokes the hieroglyph *niwt* (a circle with an *x* in the middle, symbolizing a crossroads), meaning "city."

It was above all the religious precinct and the principal temple that underwent the most extensive transformations (Fig. 13). The temple, which had been rather narrow at about 13 meters, was enlarged by 50 meters; it was flanked on the north by an apse comparable to the one in the funerary temple K XI of Classic Kerma. An entire complex was built in phases (Bonnet and Valbelle 2014, 16–28), set apart by a temenos of which the northeastern portion was uncovered. The brick wall of the temenos was 0.40 meters thick. Two foundation deposits composed of vessels completely filled with red and yellow ochre were found. The foundations of two rectangular brick chapels were preserved inside the space defined by the temenos. Further south we uncovered a building whose tripartite plan recalled that of certain chapels in the secondary urban complex. Built right up against the temple was a one-roomed rectangular chapel distinctive for its floor coated in red ochre. Visible over an extensive surface, it is still an impressive sight today. Red ochre, ground in small mortars with cylindrical pestles, was widely used in incised decoration of vessels and played a part in rituals performed next to offering tables in the chapels.

Additional chapels were founded west of what we consider to be the first Deffufa. Square in plan, these chapels have three or four columns of wood or stone on circular bases of dolomitic marble, aligned along the building axis. This type of stone, rarely

Fig. 12   Plan of the Middle Kerma city

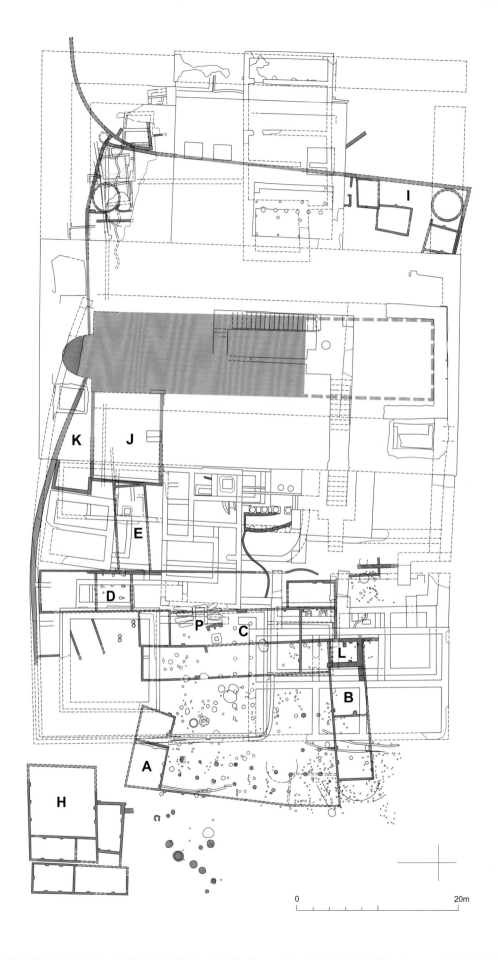

0   20m

Fig. 13 The religious precinct during Middle Kerma

used at Kerma, probably came from Third Cataract quarries, although the exact extraction site has not yet been identified. This high-quality stone, unusually white, seems to have been reserved for cult installations and the cones that capped large tumuli. In a porticoed courtyard south of the chapel, in the northwest corner of the temenos, the remains of a bronze workshop were discovered.

The large furnace of the workshop was constructed over the remnants of a previous hearth whose fire-reddened walls were preserved to a considerable depth (Bonnet and Valbelle 2004, 33–38). The workshop must have been in use for a considerable time; other subterranean facilities were observed around the furnaces (Bonnet 1986, 19–22). The principal feature consisted of a vaulted fire chamber set over eight parallel ducts, each one serving as a hearth. The ducts, oriented toward the prevailing winds, were used for draft and could be partially sealed with brick. The material recovered from the furnace, including crucibles and several mold fragments, indicate that this fire chamber was used to melt metal before pouring it into molds. This type of furnace is not typical of the Nile Valley; there are no similar

examples until the New Kingdom, at the site of Qantir in the Delta (Push 1991, 201–202).

A long covered passage was probably rebuilt in Middle Kerma above older remains. The passage bordered the north-south axis road, beginning immediately north of the entrance to the religious precinct. A double row of columns continued for more than 20 meters. The column bases were of light yellow sandstone for one of the rows; the other row was of a darker brown sandstone. This ceremonial way led to the Early Kerma complex, where a large square chamber may have hosted receptions. We have identified this complex as a palace from where the king could access the principal temple on ceremonial occasions. We must emphasize that in this period the ceremonial palace was outside the temenos; it is not until later that it was located inside the religious precinct itself.

The royal quarters were transformed with the addition of new domestic structures. The courtyard of the principal dwelling was converted into a large apartment, and adjoining structures were leveled. It is worth noting that during this period the king had another residence at his disposal in the secondary

Fig. 14   A royal audience hall

urban complex. There, too, the buildings were on a grand scale, with kitchens and service areas in a courtyard between the two buildings. They followed the typical Nubian layout of two building complexes separated by a courtyard. This plan, adopted by the monarchy, doubtless served as a model since it was frequently used throughout the city. In the urban center, the royal audience hall was renovated in several stages; its rectangular interior with rounded corners was rebuilt several times on an ever-larger scale (Fig. 14). We identified at least four expansions at the foundation level. Exterior enclosures surrounded this great structure. The light superstructure of the roof was supported by stakes along the perimeter of the building (Bonnet and Valbelle 2014, 170–173).

The architecture of the structure that served as an audience hall was quite elaborate and represented a different, less familiar tradition. Certainly there existed a local tradition dating back to prehistoric times that continued in the form of round structures serving as dwellings. South of the religious precinct, a sector much smaller in scale yielded successive strata with, in each level, hundreds of postholes delimiting circles, providing evidence of continuous occupation of the site from Early through Classic Kerma. The prehistoric tradition, which continued throughout the history of the kingdom, did not necessarily derive from the south. The audience hall, however, belonged to a different tradition whose intermediate phases are as yet unknown. The evolution of this building style remains to be explained.

The city developed progressively in independent districts that could each be closed off with its own gate. The fortified enclosure surrounding the city surmounted a series of ditches reaching 7 meters in depth. Defensive works took up more and more space. Several locations devoted to the stockpiling of goods as well as animal enclosures were established. Several of the cult annexes were moved outside the religious precinct. Fragments of oblong molds have been found scattered in ash deposits near the furnaces and silos. The large dwelling of an official was located next to workshops that occupied the vast courtyards provided for the purpose.

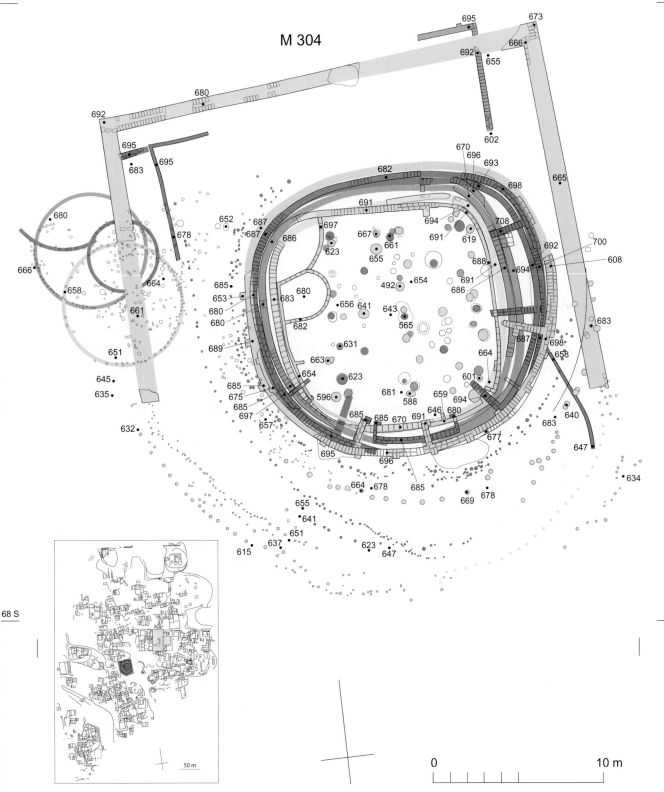

M 304

The larger dwellings were generally located along the access roads to the urban center. There is evidence of an extensive system for monitoring the passage of goods into and out of the city. House plans evolved, but the houses of the more prominent inhabitants followed the royal example with its Nubian layout. Still numerous were the single-roomed houses of Middle Kerma type, sometimes expanded with the addition of a small room. The northeast quarter of the city appears to have been reserved for smaller plots with modest homes. In the eastern quarter, building plans were more spacious and diversified. A common plan consisted of two identical rooms side by side, with an entrance on the south side and a connecting doorway on the opposite corner. This type of structure, often called a "snail house," was frequent. Another common plan was an elongated building adjoining a square room, sometimes with a vestibule providing entry to both rooms (Bonnet 1985, 11–12).

Although an interior courtyard between two buildings of a dwelling was a regular feature, much activity took place in the exterior courtyard. In the latter we found kitchens, shelters for small livestock, and round grain silos. A separate courtyard was located to the south. Its roughly oval layout delimited a 30-by-20-meter space with a circular building and a small three-room building at the north end (Bonnet and Valbelle 2014, 48–49, 142–144). These structures, African in style, may have belonged to a different population charged with guarding the activities in the courtyard, which was equipped with silos as well as a workshop framed by wooden structures. Subsequently, square shelters were added to the south side of the courtyard, probably to house additional watchmen. Such supervision can be found everywhere, as the enclosures were maintained and frequently modified. Small square buildings lining the streets, most likely guardrooms, also played a role in the protection of public installations.

The secondary urban complex became a permanent construction site as chapels were founded or rebuilt over earlier buildings (Bonnet and Valbelle 2014, 181–204). The chapels were constructed of mudbrick with a single or triple colonnade along the long axis (Fig. 15a and b). Some of the chapels opened onto a peristyle courtyard with columns placed very close to the walls. One of these chapels, surprisingly, had in front of it a hypostyle hall measuring 10 meters in length with at least three rows of wooden supports; the column bases were of compacted silt, sometimes edged with small rounded slabs of dolomitic marble. Adjoining this chapel with its hypostyle hall, a long room housed a bronze workshop with a pit furnace. Still later two bakeries were built one after the other, each with five ovens in a row. Small silos supplied the grain.

Next to this complex, another room measuring almost 10 by 6 meters had a roof supported by three rows of columns, reconstructed from their pits. The lateral walls were supported by pilasters. Almost in the center of the room was a table, probably for cult offerings. Oval in shape and measuring 0.60 by 0.10 meters, it was constructed of compacted silt. This room, separate from the neighboring workshops, must have been heavily used, as it was often rebuilt. To the south, an enormous circular oven 6 meters in diameter contained ten parallel hearths. This feature was certainly a bakery, as it was located in an enormous storage area where both bread molds and a grain silo were found. Other ovens were discovered alongside, protected by lightweight shelters. The large number of bakeries, both here and in the main city, is surprising. They were doubtless devoted to the preparation of bread offerings; other offerings would have included meat and beer.

In an extension of the secondary urban complex several buildings were excavated. Their courtyards accommodated small craft production. Several abandoned Neolithic handaxes and areas of debitage were associated with these buildings. Further to the north, an intriguing construction open on all four sides was placed next to a more isolated facility. This Classic Kerma building complex is superimposed over the older walls of a building that must certainly have served the same function. We assume that, already in the Middle Kerma period, this location was used as a goldsmith's and bronze workshop. This artisanal activity also allows us to associate the secondary urban complex with the preparation of tomb offerings.

Fig. 15a   General plan of the secondary urban complex from Early Kerma to Classic Kerma

738

745

732

753

752

749

765

742

757

808

757

740

756

781

773

772

E XII

786

774

764

762

789

E XI

E XV

782

785

795

E I

802

815

E X

M 314

821

808

760

804

770

788

770

844

871

863

858

762

889

778

760

757

854

873

748

784

740

E XIII

806

730

813

660

810

755

804

734

E VII

781

E VIII

738

712

759

E VI

E IX

M 309

E III

E V

50 m

0   10 m

Fig. 15b   General plan of the secondary urban area

It was probably the production of these offerings, and of other even more valuable grave goods, that prompted the fortification of this urban area. The east side was strongly fortified by a retaining wall and firmly founded bastions. A remarkable bastion was located on the south side, against the interior of the wall. Postholes outlined a 20-meter arc enclosing an underground area, probably used as a refuge for troops. Although the upper part of this structure was missing, it was possible to reconstruct a platform for archers. Additional pits and rectilinear walls were also part of this fortification, which extended beyond the area of excavation. A palm grove obliterated the rest of this urban area, so we will never know its full extent.

This urban complex established during the Early Kerma period belonged to an institution that lasted until the end of Classic Kerma. Its chapels and workshops were exceptionally well protected, and the influence of the Egyptian institution of *hwt-ka* (lit. "mansion [temple] of the *ka* [soul]" = place to commemorate a deceased ruler or other important individual) is obvious. On the desert route to the south, in the oasis of Balat, tripartite *hwt-ka* built

by the governors of Pepi II may have provided the model for delegations from Kerma. Although separated from the city, the religious precinct of the secondary urban area was closely integrated into the overall urban complex. Several roads must have served it from the southern quarters of the main city, where the buildings and streets are oriented in that direction.

Upon further examination of the north-south axis associated with the urbanization of the main city, it became obvious that shifting the entry to the north permitted the building of a new gate, defended by impressive fortifications (Fig. 12). On one side, a wall with connected bastions faced several massive structures; the latter included retaining walls that had been refaced several times. Only the foundations of what must have been substantial towers remain. The narrow entry passage, located at a slightly lower level, was only 0.70 meters wide. The entire northeast section of the gate was subsequently remodeled to include a rectangular platform supported by a longitudinal wall. On the south side, a spur of the alluvial terrace formed an immense rounded base, 40 meters in diameter, where there were traces, much eroded by the wind, of a chain of military works.

South of the gate, the fortifications were increased tenfold along the north-south road. Walls with connected bastions faced a series of fortifications constructed of rounded earthworks, separated every 10 meters by a thick partition wall. This defensive system was probably much more elaborate along the north-south road. The *galous* foundation of a surprising and totally unique small fort, probably added later, was preserved above these enormous bastions. This fortified building measured 11 by 8 meters, with a rectangular enclosure wall supported by nineteen slightly projecting bastions measuring 1.40 meters. Actual turrets surmounted the corners. The height of this construction must have provided the soldiers with sufficient protection against projectiles. Its entrance was on the south side, followed by a stairway up to a terrace where the garrison was located. The ivory handle of a bronze dagger had been lost in the stairway. This prestigious object must have belonged to one of the garrison commanders.

This fortified building represents a type of defensive architecture that is as yet poorly understood. Egyptian and Near Eastern reliefs show fortifications with quadrangular redans surmounted by rounded merlons. The example discussed here, with its series of rounded structures made of *galous*, belonged to an African rather than Egyptian tradition, as did all the walls with connected bastions. There existed a duality at Kerma, in this kingdom in transition between two worlds, where Nubian traditions combined as easily with influences from the south as they did with those of Egypt to the north.

Continuing along the axis road, another building appears to have been contemporary with the small fort. This building measured 4 meters wide by at least 7 meters long and was almost entirely open on one of its long sides. Numerous similar buildings have been interpreted, given their position, as military barracks. They are located primarily to the south, behind the fortification walls dominating the north-south axis road, and also among the military works that overlook the sunken entrance of the western gate. The dimensions of these barracks depended upon the number of soldiers quartered there, which must have varied from one period to the next and one fortified point to the next.

Opposite the military buildings along the north-south road, an extraordinary fortified complex raises the question of why such extensive defenses were necessary for a road in the interior of the city. We were able to follow two sections of wall for a distance of 25 meters. From the levels of collapse along the wall, we conclude that it turned the corner to form a square fortification. This remarkable complex had walls with massive circular constructions approximately 3 meters in diameter. These structures were either erected on the surface or in shallow foundation trenches. Postholes on the scraped surface indicated that the structures were anchored with wooden stakes. *Galous* was used for the foundation levels. The remains of one or two large buildings with straight walls supported by pilasters, reminiscent of garrisons, were found inside this small fortress.

This fortified complex was certainly strategically located. On one side it flanked the north-south road, facilitating surveillance of traffic; on the other, it dominated a secondary route in a small valley, obviously important judging by numerous rebuildings of the terraces protecting it. In its initial stages this road into the urban center appeared to be associated with a large bakery. At the opening of the valley, inside the gate and located at a slightly lower level, we uncovered an impressive series of ovens, with at least thirty-eight hearths arranged on either side of a central path. This bakery complex was certainly capable of producing large quantities of bread, destined perhaps, at least in part, as temple offerings. Large storerooms and additional workshops soon transformed this area. The entire ensemble would disappear and the secondary gate would be incorporated into other fortifications, including a square tower.

On the south side of the north-south axis, not too far from the audience hall, a double crossroads accommodated east-west traffic as well as a gate leading to domestic quarters. Thick *galous* walls replaced the wooden fences of previous phases. Still farther south, oval heaps of ash (0.80 by 0.40 meters) of variable height indicated the location of large pottery workshops of Early Kerma; the imprints of vessels sunk into the embers are still visible. In the collapsed levels of Middle Kerma, we found fragments of an offering table of hardened silt over a layer of red ochre. The crudely incised silhouette of an elephant was still visible on the surface of the offering plaque. The cult installation was oval, an unusual shape for Kerma. Excavations in this area yielded a large number of seal impressions, blocks of sealing clay ready for stamping, and a pyramidal seal incised with a design reminiscent of an Egyptian *serekh* (hieroglyphic symbol comprising the recessed paneling currently described as "palace-façade" decoration, modeled on the design of the earliest royal residences): a double door frame surmounted by oval arrow slits. The seal was subsequently taken out of commission by incising two lines across its surface. These discoveries may indicate that the southern gateway into the city was located just beyond the limits of our excavation.

The substantial walls that protected the structures next to the crossroads as well as the military installations nearby indicate, once again, the need to guard the entire length of the north-south road. Small square structures serving as guardhouses were also constructed near passageways. Equally noteworthy were wooden formworks for the purpose of directing water flow. While not quite as elaborate as the northern sector, this southern part of the city was very well fortified and its traffic monitored. The desire to isolate the different sectors is clear; this fragmentation may indicate hierarchical divisions within the city.

The northeast temple was completely reconstructed, replacing a building 5 meters square with a structure measuring almost 7 meters to a side (Fig. 11). The remains of mudbrick walls appear to be related to building annexes, almost entirely obliterated by wind erosion. During the first phase of Middle Kerma, the colonnade was slightly curved toward the east. Several meters farther north of the temples, double pits contained blocks of sealing clay, stored in a humid environment ready for use. The proximity of this complex to the religious precinct would appear to confirm that the cult was associated with an institution. Indeed, the seal impressions inventoried throughout the area indicate that goods passed through this point. This administrative sector was no doubt connected to the track that we discovered leading in the direction of Dukki Gel.

The almost circular temenos, originally 30 meters in diameter, was enlarged during Middle Kerma to a diameter of 46 meters, then expanded once again

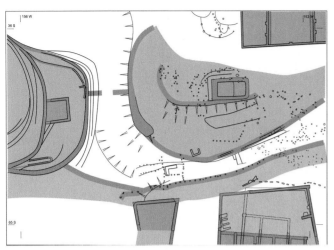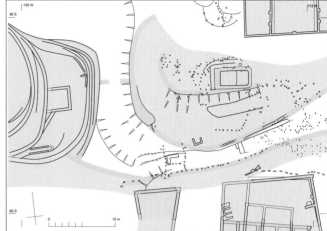

Fig. 16   The great western gate during Middle Kerma and Classic Kerma

to approximately 50 meters. Taking advantage of a slight natural hill, the temple was visible on the horizon and marked a stop along the route into the ceremonial city. The traces of only two foundation features were found, but we can infer that the temenos was already equipped with a series of semicircular buttresses, as was the case in later phases. On the west side, a rectangular construction of fired brick, a material not often found in late Middle Kerma, must have belonged to a military structure defending the northern access to the urban center. This construction surmounted a series of ditches whose slopes were reinforced by barriers blocking possible attack.

We have already stressed the careful attention lavished on the various fortifications of the Middle Kerma period, and it is probably the western gate that best illustrates these defensive efforts. The small valley of the entryway maintained the same depth and slope while a formidable quadrangular bastion blocked the central part of the complex (Fig. 16). Within this structure was a well serving the garrison, which included several shelters. Low walls reinforced by perpendicular buttresses also acted as barricades at the foot of the slope. The gate was completely rebuilt along monumental proportions totally unmatched by the other city gates. It is possible to identify several building phases, and it was not until Middle Kerma that the gate reached its final form.

The original angled entrance was maintained and heavily reinforced. Two massive rounded constructions, consisting of thick *galous* walls surmounted by earthworks, were erected in several phases. We can surmise that, very soon after, strong wooden beams were installed to reinforce the gate. Finally, rectangular towers were constructed atop the two lateral structures. A staggered passage inside the gate was protected by a quadrangular bastion, and storerooms were rebuilt at the end of the passage. This intentionally inconvenient passage was designed to allow constant surveillance and to impede entrance into the city by undesirable visitors.

This type of access corresponds to African entryways, as for example in the city of Kano in the nineteenth century. Thus we are far removed from Egyptian examples (Denyer 1978, 174–177). If we examine the general plan of the Middle Kerma city, we could conclude that its quadrangular dwellings

Fig. 17 Bucrania arranged around the south side of a Middle Kerma tomb

were rather comparable to those in neighboring Egypt. Both houses and roads were carefully laid out, preserving earlier plans. Certainly the orthogonal model of Middle Kingdom cities is not present, and the generally rounded enclosures of Kerma are closer to African compounds. Once again we emphasize the duality of Nubian urban architecture, inspired by traditional styles but influenced, above all, by northern practices.

It is also interesting to recall that in the necropolis, Middle Kerma tumuli reached considerable dimensions (Bonnet and Valbelle 2000, 24–36). The world of the dead reproduced the hierarchy that existed among the dwellings of the living. Imported Egyptian ceramics were numerous in certain sections of the necropolis while totally absent in others. Trade was most likely disrupted in times of conflict. Funerary customs grew more elaborate, most notably with the placement of bucrania on the south side of

the tumulus, and their number could be impressive: along the edge of a tumulus almost 40 meters in diameter, no fewer than 5,000 cattle skulls were deposited (Fig. 17) (Bonnet 1999, 67–70). The rulers of the kingdom had come to exercise exceptional power; they were often accompanied in the afterlife by members of their entourage and a portion of their treasure.

The funerary cult grew ever more complex, and next to certain tombs windbreaks were set up to accommodate reunions with the living. Chapels for funerary offerings were also found, generally located on the northwest side of the tomb. At the beginning of Middle Kerma, these buildings were very simple, measuring 3.00 by 1.50 meters. Later chapels were more elaborate, on a square plan with a support or axis colonnade. The chapel entrance was on the south side, slightly off center. The dead were placed in circular pits in a flexed or contracted position, with the head to the north. At first the bodies were laid to rest on cowhides, which were progressively replaced by wood-and-leather beds. Grave goods consisted of increasing amounts of foodstuffs, including large storage jars filled with grain. Entire sheep and goats, as well as cuts of meat of the same animals, accompanied the dead.

Middle Kerma was a period of consolidation for the institutions of the kingdom. The military comes first to mind, with its fortifications that demonstrated the evolution of military techniques and the importance of available troops. The secondary urban complex, modeled on the Egyptian *hwt-ka,* and the workshops for cult offerings underwent rapid development. Other institutions participated in a growing trade in goods. The upper classes were consolidating their power. Also noteworthy were the economic effort and labor supply required for the preparation of tombs and for funerary ceremonies that appear to have continued long after the interment of important individuals. Let us also remember that during this period, the territory of the kingdom was considerably expanded, based on the evidence of Middle Kerma ceramics found as far away as the Fifth Cataract. The capital of Kerma depended on supplies from several cities and regions, often hundreds of kilometers away. We are thus able to conclude that the centralization of the kingdom was successful.

The Classic Kerma City

During the Classic Kerma period the kingdom was at its height and the city underwent considerable transformation. Its layout was determined by buildings with more regular plans (Fig. 18). To the north a bastioned enclosure, rectilinear in shape, connected with older military areas (Bonnet and Valbelle 2014, 230–232), and to the south the fortifications were reinforced. East of the Deffufa, an artisanal and administrative quarter was added to the religious precinct. A new palace residence was constructed next to the western gate. Buildings were reconstructed and enlarged across the greater part of the city. The street layout remained the same and new gates were constructed, shifted toward the outside after the filling of some ditches. The Deffufa was enlarged and raised in elevation (Fig. 19). The entrance was through a monumental lateral gateway, square in plan, constructed on the west side of the temenos. The brickwork was particularly thick, supporting a height of almost 8 meters. This monumental construction was due to the traffic flow from the entrance hall, which also opened, on the north side, onto a double-colonnaded hall leading to the ceremonial palace (Bonnet and Valbelle 2004, 27–73). Traces of a red ochre wash were observed on the walls of the hall. Entrance into the building was up a flight of eight steps. A double-leaved wooden door served to seal off the passage. From there a staircase of twelve steps led into a room measuring 7.00 by 2.40 meters, most probably the sanctuary. This chamber opened on the east onto a narrow blind corridor oriented to the north, perhaps for the placement of cult statues or, possibly, a bark. The walls of the stairwell, like those of the hall, were originally covered in wood panels or planks that were entirely burned. In the hall itself, close to its original location, was a cylindrical stone of dolomitic marble more than 1 meter in diameter; the flawlessness of the stone as well as its precise carving suggest that it was used as an altar base. In the southeast corner, the burnt remains of bedding and layers of manure indicated the presence of small livestock. Another narrower staircase, angled at the end, led to a roof terrace 6 meters above. This access could be closed off by a door, of which burnt fragments have survived. Low brick remains probably corresponded to the foundations of a small structure, perhaps a chapel. The floor of

200 N

100 N

0.0

100 S

200 S

300 S

0   50 m

Fig. 18   Schematic plan of the Classic Kerma city

the blind corridor, repaved at least once, was covered by a network of wide coupled beams capable of supporting brickwork 4 meters high. The Deffufa, preserved to a height of 16 meters, originally measured almost 20 meters. Its southern extension was considerably higher, approximately 25 meters. Although in its final stages the plan of the Deffufa may recall that of an Egyptian temple, the southern extension, with its solid masonry and entrance on the side, did not serve the same function as an Egyptian pylon. The northern apse of the preceding building phase was incorporated into the facing that encircled the monument as a whole. The four corners were used to good effect for the erection of four small rooms whose walls were covered in ferruginous sandstone slabs. Oddly enough, no trace remains of the superstructure of these rooms; perhaps they connected to the terrace above through a shaft-like opening. The outline of the temenos was preserved and defined the western part of the religious precinct. At the end of Classic Kerma, a section of wall collapsed suddenly; since the fallen brickwork was more or less intact, it was possible to estimate the height of the wall at approximately 5 meters.

The chapel in the northwest corner of the religious precinct was square in shape with an axial colonnade. Ceramic offering vessels were embedded in the silt floor. The entrance to the chapel, located along the south wall, was defined on its east side by the banister of an exterior staircase leading to the roof, as in both Deffufas. This layout reinforces the hypothesis that a solar cult was located here, as well as a chthonian cult in the blind corridor of the main temple. To the south, a second chapel was constructed of fired brick; its axial colonnade was reconstructed from three column bases in dolomitic marble. Two side-by-side vestibules were constructed in front of this chapel. The ceremonial palace complex was also located in this quarter. This tripartite building had a large rectangular hall flanked on either side by a storeroom; porticoes and side buildings surrounded it. One of the annexes contained a well meticulously lined with ferruginous sandstone slabs. A hypostyle hall connected the palace to the entrance of the Deffufa. Stone and wood pillars rested on dolomitic marble bases; a single column drum 1 meter high, also of dolomitic marble, remained in the hall. Access at the back of the hall led

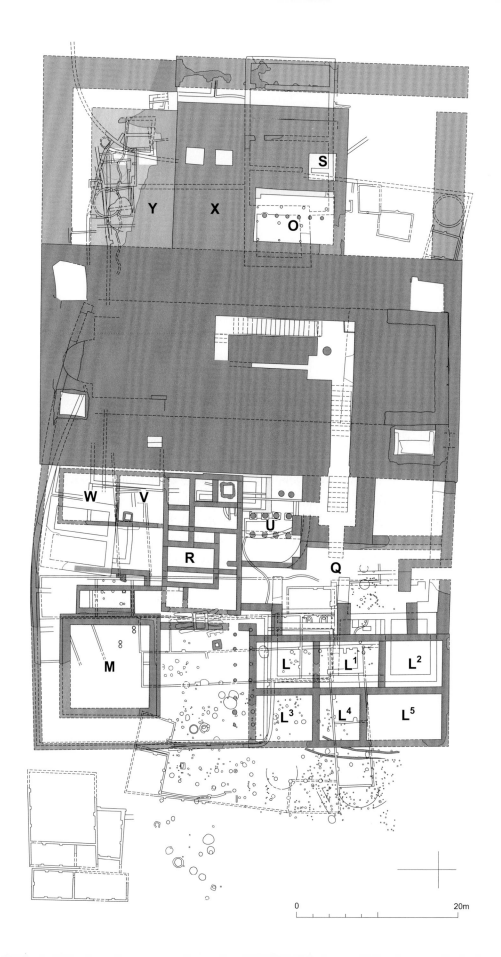

0   20m

Fig. 19   The religious precinct during Classic Kerma

to an administrative center where a square pit reinforced with stone contained blocks of sealing clay.

On the other side of the Deffufa, the temenos wall was much thicker, secluding two massive mudbrick structures in which George Reisner found storage pits for precious objects (Reisner 1923a, 23–29). These caches were pillaged and burned. A chapel was positioned in the southern structure, where the previous cultic practice of covering the floor with red ochre continued. At first the chapel was covered with a Nubian vault that apparently collapsed soon after construction. It was replaced with lighter roofing supported by a long axial colonnade on bases of dolomitic marble; its brick floor was coated with red ochre. Lastly, following the wars at the beginning of the New Kingdom and the resumption of power by a coalition led by the king of Kerma, the cult installation was restored with a roof supported by several rows of vertical beams. Traces of fire bear witness to the upheavals of this period.

Examination of the levels of the Deffufa confirms that this enormous brick complex dominating the religious precinct belonged to the end of Classic Kerma (Bonnet and Valbelle 2004, 53–59). The structure was built in layers of brick 3 to 4 meters high, stabilized with wooden frames. The brick layers are interspersed with thick layers of silt. When the kingdom was attacked, the Deffufa was set on fire and the wooden reinforcements incinerated. It is still possible to see large areas of fire-reddened brick, most notably at the ends of the beams in and around the monument. Portions of this 3,500-year-old structure have nonetheless been preserved to a considerable height.

Beyond the Deffufa, along the road leading to the northeast temple, yet another chapel was erected, this one circular in shape. Its thick wall, reinforced by two buttresses, must have served to support a considerable elevation. The floor was paved with mudbrick, and a dolomitic marble column base is still in situ in the middle of the room (Fig. 18). It is not possible to determine whether the roof was conical or flat with a slight slope since this circular plan was unique in the city. The chapel was constructed in a late period and, unlike other cult buildings, did not replace an older chapel. It appears to be aligned with the northeast temple and was not enclosed by a wall.

Fig. 20   The northeast temple during Middle Kerma
and Classic Kerma

The temenos of the northeast temple can be associated with the route leading to Dukki Gel. Its wall diameter was increased to 55 meters (Fig. 20) and it was supported by circular buttresses reminiscent of connected bastions. Two towers protected the entrance, the walls reinforced with buttresses and smaller towers. The remains of the temple and its surroundings are more complete. A side annex was added to the sanctuary, which was enclosed by a narrow wall forming what could be considered an interior temenos. Entrance into this enclosure was through a second gateway with two large circular buttresses, probably reinforced on the interior. The gateway, 3 meters wide, was protected by upright bastions. On the west side, a long and narrow courtyard housed a grain silo. To the east, a vast hall cut across the axis leading to the temple; it featured an entry porch and a small annex. The route to the sanctuary door was deflected off course because the annex stood in its way. In the northeast corner of this religious complex, hearths or bread ovens, a kneading trough, a grain silo, and a mastaba can be associated with the preparation of offerings. Several rooms that encircle the cult installation were certainly used in ceremonies honoring the god. Outside the temenos, to the northeast, two half-buried rectangular features contained blocks of sealing clay, confirming that this area continued to be used for administrative functions (Gratien 1991, 21–24; 1993, 27–32). Hundreds of seal impressions are evidence of the processing of goods in this location. Erosion has destroyed the area where outgoing goods were sealed and dispatched. On the other side, to the west, a vast quadrangular courtyard bordered on the north by a portico had a guardhouse in its center. This sector must have been reserved for the defense of the religious precinct in the secondary urban complex. The evolution of the latter also underwent modifications that included, above all, the reinforcement or rebuilding of its defenses, transforming it into a virtual fortress (Fig. 21). Inside, several chapels were rebuilt, most of them on existing locations. A gate erected on an elevation of earth became the main entrance that could only be reached by crossing a ditch that separated the secondary urban complex from the city proper. This ditch was not always filled with water, as we could see from the footprints on the narrow path leading to

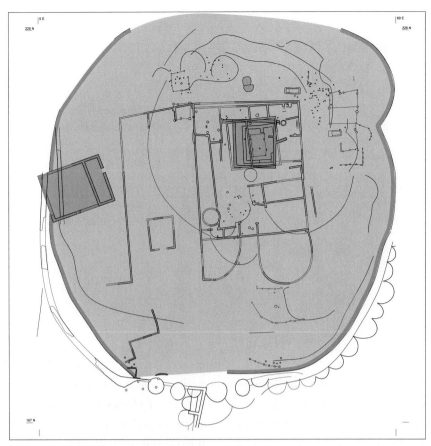

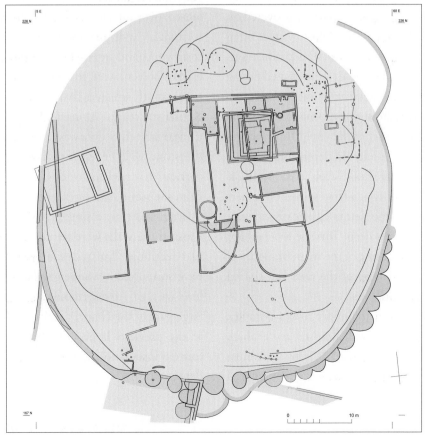

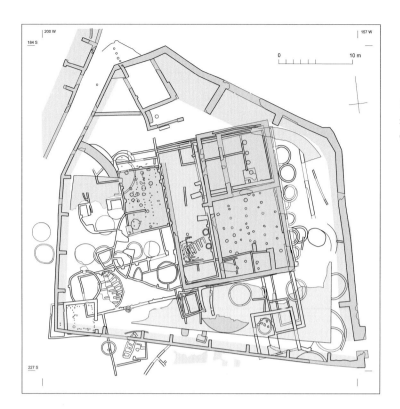

Fig. 21 The northern area of the secondary urban complex during Classic Kerma

the two moles on either side of the gateway. Another route across the ditch must have existed farther north, where a lookout post was discovered on the city side. It consisted of three narrow areas fitted into an angle at the end of a road. The fortifications of the secondary urban complex were erected taking into consideration the transverse passage. There, too, crossing the ditch without getting one's feet wet was possible only during part of the year. Our sondages in the ditch reached 7 meters in depth, and we were able to observe multiple flood levels in the sections. During building activity at a farm some 200 meters to the west, sherds of the Kerma Classic period were found almost 12 meters deep. This site was perhaps located on the bank of one of the main branches of the Nile. Today the course of the river has shifted about 1 kilometer to the east.

Along the ditch, the secondary urban complex was protected by a stone wall almost 1 meter thick (Bonnet and Valbelle 2014, 232). This wall must have been several meters high, as it was anchored

quite deeply in the soil. In the northeast corner, water undermined the stone layers, which collapsed over an area at least 4 meters wide. This formidable wall was reinforced with perpendicular formworks and interior garrison rooms. A few everyday objects were found on the floors. Along a north-south street, a bastion replaced the Middle Kerma structures. Alongside the ditch, after a rectilinear stretch, a doorway 1 meter wide opened in the stone wall. It led into a very long peripheral corridor reserved for troops. Thick walls extended from the stone structures, cutting off the northeast quarter, and only a single chapel remained in use. Most of the walls were reinforced with perpendicular rectilinear buttresses, a system that may also have supported a wooden walkway above a floor-level passage. An enormous layer of brick covered a large part of the chapel precinct as well as portions of the previous hypostyle hall. Almost all of the former installations were abandoned in favor of defense.

A bastion of considerable proportions (30 meters) was located farther south, in a neighboring quarter. We excavated several layers of brick forming semicircular platforms that supported a central tower. To the north, a thick mass of brickwork also of circular plan may indicate the presence of a second tower. The secondary urban complex was transformed into a fortress, to the detriment of some of its sanctuaries and workshops. The site adjoining the chapels was now occupied by an enormous donjon of sorts. To the south, however, the old enclosure wall was prolonged, making room for a protected sector. This enclosure followed the Middle Kerma plan and included an interior bastion 25 meters in size, supported by a thick earthwork. An underground chamber was excavated along one of the edges and a new entrance created to an older chamber. Oddly enough, a foundation deposit with miniature vases dating to the Eighteenth Dynasty was found above this bastion on the side facing the interior of the religious complex. The closest comparison is to ceramic material from a deposit of Thutmose III on Sai Island. An Egyptian temple of the New Kingdom may have existed here, but practically nothing remains.

The eastern gate into the urban area was altered during fortification work. The staggered passage was lined on both sides with tripartite buildings (Fig. 15). The north building consisted of an interior corridor leading to a doorway; to the south, a large central hall likely had an official function. Traffic flowed around the large bastion to reach an interior gate opening onto a group of three chapels of special significance. The western chapel, with its long peristyle courtyard opening onto a transverse road, was continuously renovated from Early Kerma on. It must have served to commemorate a king with a remarkable reign. The two other chapels were associated with a four-columned courtyard containing an altar. One of these sanctuaries was rebuilt and the door to the courtyard displaced laterally.

An area of workshops was located to the northwest. One of these structures, open on all four sides, was a metallurgical workshop, as indicated by fire-reddened deposits as well as slag and crucible fragments. Close by, in a small and confined room, a base may have been used for hammering. A much larger room extended to the south. It contained a pedestal measuring 1.30 meters to a side. On the

27 E
69 E
73 S
700
698
718
726
720
620
721
722
582
719
703
642
707
688
718
713
657
716
621
707
710
712
709
693
657
686
691
705
615
709
661
764
714
748
711
705
659
723
659
626
614
702
628
701
659
681
670
697
700
659
685
679
671
698
689
684
660
665
635
603
677
664
589
654
680
563
668
639
650
670
551
657
658
639
663
600
641
671
658
645
655
506
663
636
648
645
647
662
651
682
673
636
653
658
604
594
473
592
522
532
619
461
494
586
579
626
141
534
582
402
608
631
388
600
655
518
496
0
10 m
50 m
132 S

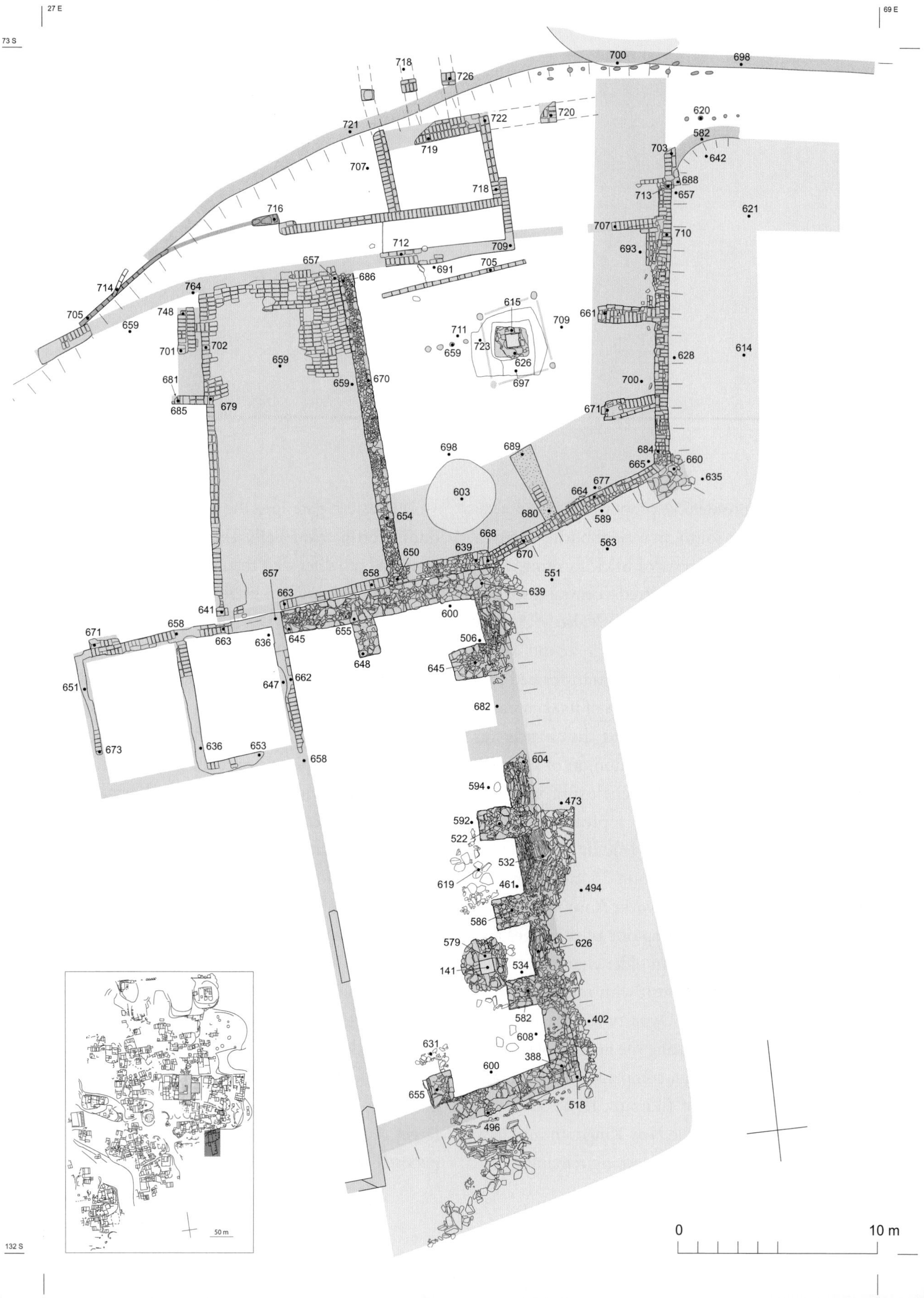

Fig. 22   The outer gate of the southern fortifications

floor, completely coated and smoothed, stake holes outlined a wooden frame probably used as a work-bench. A 4-millimeter gold ingot was found in front of the pedestal. This workshop is located not far from the two royal residences in the secondary urban complex. The network of streets was reorganized with protective walls providing more privacy for the dwellings. To the south, the extraordinary fortified gate retained its prominence. A square masonry plat-form with an access ramp was laid out on the hill and, at the foot of the hill, earthworks lined the path. Archers were thus able to observe traffic around the base of the hill. The entrance, laterally displaced, consisted of two moles, each 4 meters wide, posi-tioned on either side of a passage 0.80 meters wide prolonged by a wall. To the side and above, guard-houses rounded out the complex.

The reinforcement of the fortifications affected several sectors of the city. The most dramatic modi-fications were in the south, where a second gate was constructed in front of the existing one (Fig. 22), while a rectangular tower was erected in front of the gateway bastions, creating a staggered entry. Pillars supported an elevated passage connecting the tower to the double-bastioned gateway and providing a large platform for guards. A massive 12-meter-long structure was then erected to the south, flanked by a courtyard protected by a wall faced with fired brick firmly anchored with frameworks. Between this structure and the tower, a separate passage opened into the courtyard.

In the center of the open space, a stone well was sunk into the water table. Square in shape, it was built inside a large circular pit. At a later date a frame of four stakes was erected to support lightweight roofing. A line of posts to the west must have been part of a lifting apparatus for drawing water in a goatskin. The interior of the well, measuring 0.70 meters, was lined with thin and rather crude slabs of ferruginous sandstone arranged vertically to form a regular face. The upper surface of the exterior wall served as a lookout over the ditch that flanked the fortification wall, reinforced in one corner by a stone buttress. An angle in the wall is suggested by a pillar that supported an upper passage between the exte-rior wall and the tower.

In front of this complex, a stone wall almost 1.50 meters thick extended for nearly 28 meters, forming

Fig. 23   Clusters of ovens in the eastern bakery complex

an impressive tenaille. On its inner side the wall was supported by buttresses spaced 2 or 3 meters apart, constructed of roughly squared stone blocks from Third Cataract quarries. A second well, lined with thick stone walls, was sunk into the trapezoidal space. Built right up against the two faces of the structure were two mudbrick buildings that may have been part of the defenses, but they were too poorly preserved to yield much information. Several sondages in the ditch showed that water had undermined the foundations of the stone wall, causing the collapse of entire sections.

It is possible that the foregate was associated with the principal entry at the southern end of the axis road through the city. The addition of this gate, however, must be associated with other fortifications located elsewhere around the urban sectors. The foregate is especially interesting because its construction seems to have been inspired by Egyptian models from Mirgissa at the Second Cataract. Egyptian influence probably intensified at the end of Classic Kerma, when Nubian troops took control of territory as far as Aswan. We know that the king of Kerma had Egyptians in his service, notably in Buhen, where a temple was constructed on behalf of the Nubian ruler. We can imagine that Egyptians also participated in building activity at Kerma itself, especially in the construction of this distinctive foregate.

East of the Deffufa, a stone wall bordering the ditches outlined a prominent trapezoidal fortification related to the smaller structures of Middle Kerma. In front of the enclosure, pilasters supported compartments for archers, probably protected by partial roofing. A remarkable bridge spanned a narrow ditch, most likely an arm of the river refurbished during the short flood season. The mudbrick foundations of the bridgehead are preserved 14 meters in front of the enclosure wall. This brickwork replaced the fences of interlaced branches and posts located along the slopes of the ditch as a barrier against assailants. Well protected behind its robust stone wall, this area housed a bakery for bread offerings and an administrative building for the inventory and storage of goods arriving through the eastern gate.

A square courtyard was located in the northeast corner of the stone fortification wall. A covered portico served as an entrance vestibule; its roof was supported by three columns whose bases, covered in

red ochre, were firmly set in rectangular beds. The portico continued to the east on the other side of a partition wall. Less than 1 meter in front of the portico, an oven 14 meters long contained more than ten hearth compartments in parallel alignment (Fig. 23). Each rectangular compartment, 1.20 by 0.50 meters, was probably covered by a small vault. Several bread molds were found in some of the hearths, some of which were still positioned for baking in the coals. Near the center of the courtyard was a square well 1 meter to a side, dressed with ferruginous sandstone slabs. Other porticoes for the preparation of dough were located in the opposite corner. The roofing material of palm fibers was laid over beams supported by oblong pillars. Against the stone wall, a rectangular chamber with walls of mixed stone and brick still had, in its center, a circular base of dolomitic marble for a single column. The care taken in the construction of this special room suggests that it functioned as a chapel.

Given the large quantity of cattle bones found near the hearths, the bakery complex was probably also used for the preparation of other food offerings. The workrooms continued south of the courtyard, where, at a deeper level, we cleared a small vaulted building with two pillars in front, probably a cellar. Most of the bread molds were cone-shaped with a flat base or, less frequently, tapered to a point (Jacquet-Gordon 1981). This large bakery, which replaced earlier workshops located in or near the central religious precinct, must have served an establishment associated with the Deffufa. The layout of the bakery, like its dimensions, reflects the increase in production required to support the activities of the temple and chapels. A large administrative building, perhaps associated with the bakery complex, was located nearby. On either side of a central alleyway, a series of square storerooms were certainly intended for the storage of goods. In the enormous plaza to the south, sacks, chests, and bundles were opened and their contents sorted. Sealing and preparation for shipment probably took place in the alley and a room at its eastern end. Associated features and a well were located in the middle of the building, whose walls had been rearranged several times. Near the eastern gate of the city, a portico of sorts opened onto the plaza, constructed of two rooms that formed the moles of the entry. Thousands of seal impressions dating to Middle or Classic Kerma were found while clearing the plaza (Gratien 1991, 21–24; 1993, 27–32). Several seals from the same deposits were engraved with simple geometric or hieroglyphic motifs. These objects were located in an area of some importance, controlled by guards who were housed in a small square structure built on an elevation.

The larger dwellings were probably connected to the road network and the city gates. With their spacious exterior courtyards, these residences were most likely reserved for officials in charge of the traffic of goods. Another class of the city's residents must have lived in circular houses, sometimes grouped in separate quarters or exterior courtyards. The large houses follow the traditional Nubian plan almost exclusively. Wall collapse allowed us to reconstruct

pilastered walls from 3.50 to 4 meters in height. Small pillars generally raised the flat roof above the tops of the walls, letting in a welcome flow of air during the hot seasons. In wintertime branches would seal the 30-centimeter openings above the walls.

During the Classic Kerma period, the small valley of the western entrance gradually filled with debris (Bonnet and Valbelle 2014, 165–167), making the area available for the unusual palace residence of one of the last kings of Kerma (Fig. 24). Its main walls are aligned according to two vanishing points: the principal chapel of the secondary urban complex to the south and the entrance courtyard of the Deffufa to the east. Thus the palace was under the protection of the main god of the city as well as the guardianship of a former king. The plan was original, without any comparison to date. The entrance was on the west, most likely right after the city gate. To the north, one proceeded down a long corridor; two-thirds of the way along the length of the building, it turned at a right angle toward a narrow doorway only 0.70 meters wide, constricted by a large pillar. This doorway led to a vestibule

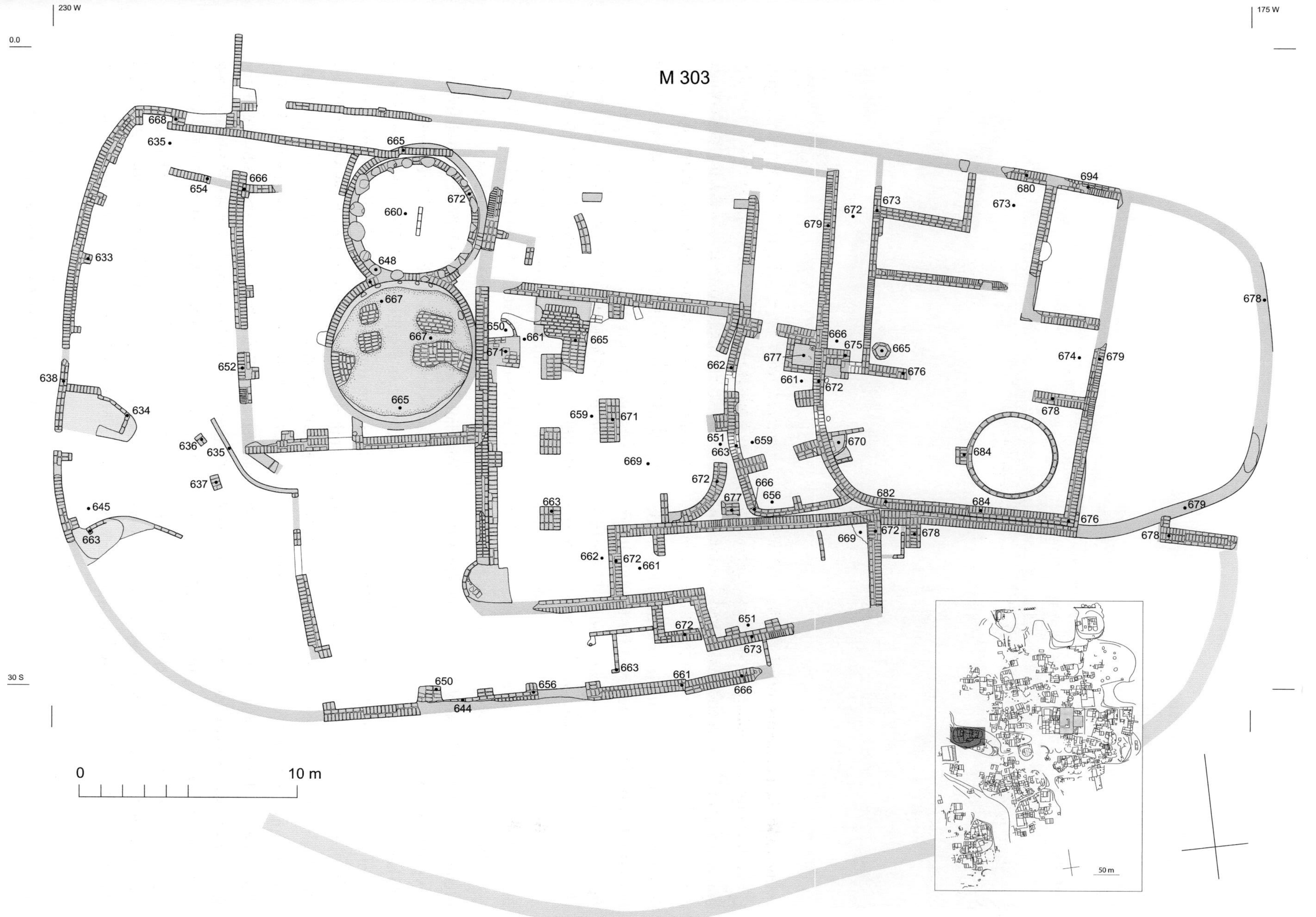

M 303

Fig. 24   The palace at the end of Classic Kerma

with curving walls. Two additional doorways, one of which may have been reserved for the sole use of the king, opened into the throne room. In the vestibule was a square basin containing several thousand blocks of sealing clay; this area must have been used for the sealing of royal messages. Adjoining the vestibule was a small room that may be interpreted as an archive, analogous to examples in Egyptian fortresses.

The throne room measured 15 by 11 meters, with a roof supported by heavy rectangular pillars of brick. Two areas were probably separated by a light partition wall. The first area, with its semicircular bench, functioned as a waiting room for visitors. The throne itself was placed along the north wall of the second area on a platform preceded by a ramp; on either side were found traces of hearths and a location for a water jar. Oddly enough, the platform was aligned with the roof-support pillars, compelling the architect to provide a second platform

alongside the row of pillars. The king was thus able to change his seat and deal with another group of people in the western bay of the room. South of this complex, a room opened into another section of the palace containing two large grain silos, each 7 meters in diameter, as well as livestock enclosures (Fig. 25). Small features in the courtyard were probably associated with the care of livestock. Two defensive structures on either side of the entrance to the palace indicate that a military contingent was housed on site. From the south wall, reinforced by pilasters, guards were able to monitor the expanse of gardens on the neighboring property. The east side of the palace contained apartments of several rooms each as well as a porticoed terrace. A grain silo, a granary on the terrace, and a kneading trough provided the food supply for residents in this part of the palace, who also had access to a large rounded courtyard.

Shortly before the city was abandoned, a final complex was built in a central quarter, south of the

Fig. 25   The Classic Kerma palace after restoration

royal residences. The main residence had an unusual plan, consisting of a large rectangular hall with a colonnade along the long axis and two rooms on either side of a central stairway. The building had an upper floor, as suggested by the 1-meter-thick foundation. This dwelling, unique in the city, was constructed at the same time as a second one to the south, on the other side of a courtyard. The three rooms of the second house were simple but carefully built. Since some of the buff-colored pottery vessels found inside date to the New Kingdom, it is possible that these structures continued to be occupied after the city was largely abandoned.

At the time of its abandonment, the ancient city of Kerma was the capital of a kingdom at its peak. After the Egyptian conquest, the principal temple was burned and the inhabitants deserted the city. According to research conducted by Brigitte Gratien at Gism el-Arba, farming villages and hamlets in the hinterland continued to be occupied and some activities were centralized. Equally noteworthy was

the growing number of settlements during this period. While Derek Welsby may have found in Wadi el-Khowi, several dozen kilometers away, evidence of a climatic shift that caused an increased scarcity of water (Welsby 2001), the urbanization of Dukki Gel was hardly in decline; on the contrary, activity during the reigns of the Eighteenth Dynasty pharaohs was considerable, and local labor must have been involved. The abandonment must therefore have been the result, in large part, of the conflicts at the beginning of the New Kingdom. The Deffufa was not razed, but the cult was no longer maintained. At Dukki Gel, on the other hand, some of the native sanctuaries remained in use, their activities apparently permitted by the Egyptian occupants. Henceforth it was this ceremonial city that became the Nubian or African religious center. The gods of the Egyptian pantheon were included in this revival, as the Egyptians established at Dukki Gel a religious center dedicated to Amun of Pnubs.

The Port Area and Temple

Almost 1 kilometer south of the ancient city (Bonnet and Valbelle 2014, 209–214), we conducted a rescue excavation in an artisanal quarter of the modern city, in a center devoted to the production of olive oil. The remains of an extensive administrative complex were discovered close to the surface. The material recovered indicates a long period of occupation (Fig. 26). Ceramics from an early phase of Middle Kerma, the stone walls of a Classic Kerma building, and an abundance of finds raise the possibility that this complex belonged to a port on a fossil riverbed. Because of modern habitation, we were not able to clear the entire area, but the great number of seal impressions confirms that a considerable exchange of goods must have taken place. As indicated by seals from the Middle Kingdom and the Second Intermediate Period, some of the merchandise may have originated in Egypt.

More than a century ago Karl R. Lepsius surveyed the site and identified a dike along the river as well as stone circles belonging to a necropolis (Lepsius 1913, 245–247). His observations have been partially verified, and it is reasonable to assume that an important settlement was founded along the extensions of the former islands of Kerma and Dukki Gel. Large islands such as Argo, for example, only a few kilometers away, have helped us understand how vast alluvial terraces were isolated or shaped into promontories by the arms of the Nile. Local inhabitants confirm that seasonal inundations flooded this area without reaching the remains located on higher ground. The main course of the river was brought under control in ancient times and an earthen levee protected the urban areas.

This settlement, interpreted as a port, was established behind an earthen dike that was probably artificial, first mentioned by Lepsius. The original settlement was identified from grain pits associated with hundreds of postholes; a few rare Early Kerma potsherds were found within. Slightly later, a surprisingly large circular structure 10.60 meters in diameter was constructed; it had few equivalents in the ancient city itself. Rebuilt at least twice on virtually the same spot, this structure may have been used for the storage of goods. Other circular constructions were located close to the initial complex. Modern fencing in the area under study prevented us from continuing excavation in the

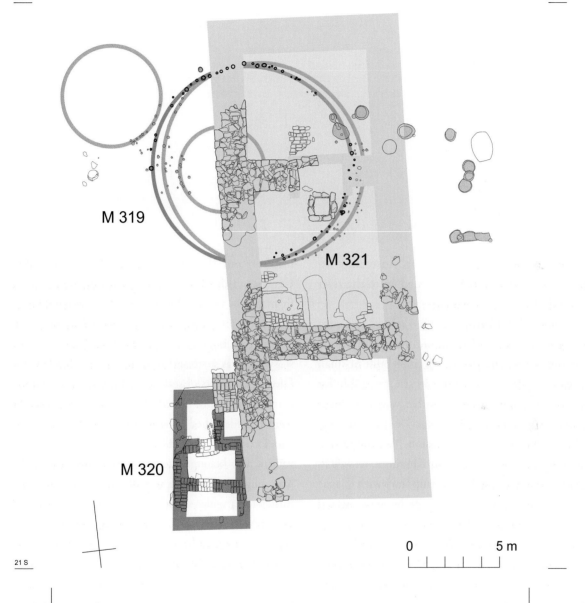

10 W

16 E

9 N

M 319

M 321

M 320

21 S

0   5 m

Fig. 26   The port quarter with its administrative building

Fig. 27   The temple and chapel in the port quarter

direction of the Nile, but we can reasonably assume that the settlement continued up to the river and its dike.

A mudbrick building 7.50 by 4 meters was subsequently erected south of the round buildings. Its four rooms were equipped with units built of small mudbricks 8 by 5 centimeters in size, probably for the storage of precious objects that were no longer present; only seal impressions survive. Brigitte Gratien, who analyzed the impressions, identified several examples from the Middle Kingdom, as well as two seals of Hyksos rulers contemporary with Classic Kerma. These storerooms were perhaps connected to an earlier brick building, replaced during the Classic Kerma period, at which time the storerooms themselves were also modified. Access was from above, from the neighboring building. Thus we are dealing with hidden and protected shafts constructed. A large buttress on the west side completed the complex.

The Kerma Classic building comprised two square rooms 5 meters to a side, placed on either side of a large quadrangular hall 7 meters long. The exceptionally thick walls included roughly shaped blocks from the Tumbus quarries of the Third Cataract. This type of masonry was mainly used for fortification works. We can therefore conclude that valuable merchandise was stored in this carefully constructed building, which probably had an upper story and was surrounded by annexes. A shallow well filled with blocks of sealing clay confirms its administrative function. Paved floors and other features were also identified. A cult building of considerable size, located a mere 100 meters away on a slight elevation, also belonged to the port district (Fig. 27). The religious structure was on the same site as an earlier rectangular wooden building almost 20 meters long, identified by several rows of postholes slightly misaligned with the later walls. Excavation was not conducted in depth, but it certainly would be interesting to continue work in this area, as additional rows of postholes indicate that the site was already occupied in Early Kerma.

The temple that succeeded the earlier wooden structure was built on mudbrick foundations from which we were able to reconstruct the plan: a transverse vestibule opening into three elongated rooms, further extended by an enclosed space. In front of

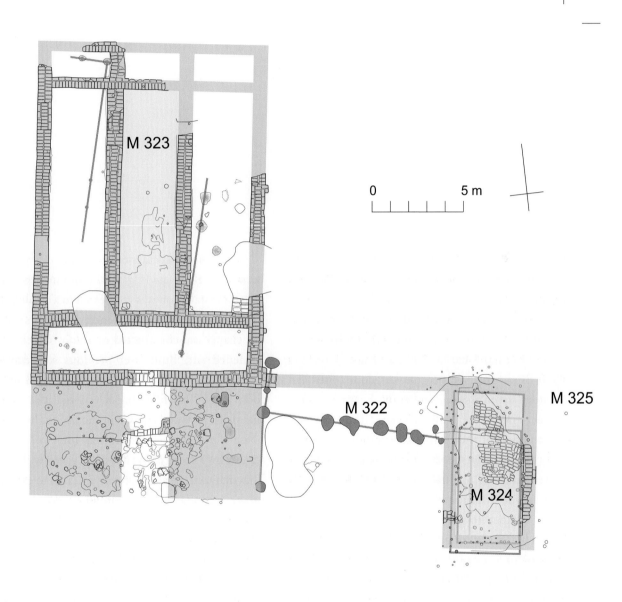

M 323

M 322

M 325

M 324

0   5 m

Fig. 28   The temple in the port quarter

the vestibule were found several stones from two massive square structures, most likely a pylon of sorts. Egyptian models from the early New Kingdom may have directly influenced this tripartite plan, but the ceramic material found within belonged to Classic Kerma, dated in this case to approximately 1500 BCE. The rulers of the kingdom controlled territory up to Aswan, and some Egyptians were subservient to the Nubian rulers. The plan and construction of the temple are reminiscent of the sanctuary of Hatshepsut in Buhen, which was moved from its original location to the National Museum in Khartoum. The temple also calls to mind another religious building from an earlier period before the conquest by Thutmose I, built for the king of Kerma by the commander Sepedhor in honor of the god Horus (Smith et al. 1976, 80 et seq.). We have already alluded to Egyptian influence, noticeable in the main city and its fortifications and particularly evident in the port district. Import and export of goods via the Nile were subject to the difficulties of transport due to the natural barriers of the cataracts to the north, which hardly favored navigation.

The religious precinct of the port appears to have been quite elaborate (Fig. 28). From its beginnings the cult installation was connected to a small chapel by a substantial wooden fence. In its first phase the chapel was constructed of acacia branches and hardened silt. Built over previous structures, it measured 6 by 3.40 meters and consisted of one room only. This first chapel was replaced by two slightly larger wood chapels in succession. In its final phase a mudbrick building was built on a larger scale, 9 by 5 meters. The floor was paved with brick. This architectural development is similar to examples in the secondary urban complex, where wooden chapels were likewise replaced with larger brick structures.

After abandonment the religious complex was replaced by an extensive necropolis that extended to the north, close to the location of a circular animal pen (*zeriba*), identifiable from the hoofprints of cattle as well as traces of its thorn enclosure. Potsherds date this feature to the Kerma period. A New Kingdom cemetery of a population of modest means was partly identified as well. The contracted or flexed positions of the deceased confirm that they were

indigenous to the region; local funeral customs were obviously resistant to Egyptianization. The shallow pits probably had a superstructure of side walls with a thicker wall, at the head of the deceased, supporting a Nubian vault. Due to the friable state of the skeletal remains, it was impossible to remove them for anthropological study. Dark stains in the soil did, however, suggest the presence of fabric, and the position of several adults may indicate that they were tightly contracted inside bags. Cords may have bound their legs and arms against the body. Grave goods included objects of local manufacture: crude hemispherical bowls and carinated vases with narrow necks, red on the outside and black on the inside. Egyptian imports were also found: buff-colored ovoid jars with two or three handles, red-slip plates, New Year's flasks (also known as "pilgrim flasks"), calcite vases, jasper earrings, and bronze vessels. Based on comparisons with similar grave goods from Soleb, this ensemble may be dated to the middle of the New Kingdom.

This necropolis continued in use during the Napatan and Meroitic periods. Although we were unable to excavate the entire sector, as it was partially covered with modern houses, it was possible to observe, in plazas and in several streets, cemeteries of varying density. We identified two types of inhumations belonging to the Napatan period following Egyptian occupation: some bodies were contracted and buried with rich grave goods, and others were extended in a coffin with no goods at all. Once again, the traditional customs of local Kerma cultures coexisted with Egyptian-style coffin burials. As early as 1923, after his excavations in the cemetery at Sanam near modern Kareima, F. L. Griffith pointed out this duality of funeral customs: royal and noble tombs belonged to an Egyptianized population, while the middle class long remained true to its indigenous roots (Griffith 1923, 73–171). Kerma may mark a southern limit, as this dual tradition has not been observed in Lower Nubia.

Of the forty tombs studied, only a quarter belonged to the Nubian tradition (Bonnet 1995, 50–52). Besides ceramics, the grave goods in these pit burials included scarabs, amulets, a few objects of iron (knives) and bronze (razors), and jewelry of faience or glass beads. Most notable was an exquisite enameled flask of local manufacture. The coffin burials were placed in vaults dug into the alluvial soil, accessible by a descending stepped passage. A fairly deep bowl covered in red slip was sometimes left in front of the vault door, part of a rite performed at the end of the burial ceremony. Despite the considerable state of decay of the wood, some coffins retained traces of brightly colored decoration. Two female bodies were covered with a bead fillet depicting a face bordered by geometric motifs. These tubular faience beads in different colors were retrieved by the hundreds from the coffins.

During Meroitic times, from the fourth century BCE to the fourth century CE, the cemeteries extended over a considerable area, from the entire site of the ancient city of Kerma to the city of Dukki Gel and the port. Reisner excavated a large sector in the northwest, 800 meters from the Deffufa. Systematic excavation was not possible and, given the state of the research, it is difficult to provide a complete analysis of this necropolis. Only a few Classical Meroitic tombs were cleared, either next to the temple precinct of the port or 1,500 meters to the north, in an area directly threatened by agricultural expansion. The large descending passages located in the ancient city northwest of the Deffufa appear to have belonged to important local personages. The square foundations of the mudbrick pyramids surmounting the tombs have, in places, escaped complete erosion. They were probably between 5 and 10 meters in height. Although most of the vaults were extensively looted, the few remaining objects exemplify the high quality of the grave goods. Some of the ceramics are particularly noteworthy for their fine clay and variety of decoration, easily distinguishable from the production of other workshops in the Nile Valley. Also noteworthy are rare items of jewelry, such as beautiful crescent-shaped earrings of gold.

One of the tombs north of the Deffufa deserves special mention. The burial vault was associated with a neighboring tomb and must have been topped by a pyramid almost entirely leveled in modern times. A Nubian vault covered the burial chamber, which measures 6 by 1.80 meters. This is the largest Meroitic tomb discovered to date at Kerma. Thirteen individuals—seven infants, an adolescent, and five adults—were extended on their backs, oriented east-west with the head to the west. Among the modest grave goods, a typical Classic Meroitic jar, a bronze bowl, and a small tin-plated bronze chalice were probably used for purification rites or libations. It is not uncommon to find sherds of a bowl, intentionally broken at the conclusion of funerary rites, outside the door of the funerary chamber at the bottom of the descending passage. Amulets, including one in the shape of a ram's head; beads of gilded glass, faience, and carnelian; tweezers; and an iron arrowhead round out the inventory, dated to the end of the first century BCE or the century following. This tomb probably belonged to a single family.

Equally noteworthy is the tomb of a priest of Amun of Pnubs excavated in the courtyard of a school located at the southern edge of the ancient city (Bonnet and Valbelle 1980, 3–12). The layout of the Meroitic cemetery has led us to conclude

that this tomb was the earliest one in the area. It was, unfortunately, disturbed; only one end of both the chamber and the anthropomorphic coffin was found in situ. Consisting of wooden planks covered with painted plaster, the narrow vault was almost entirely occupied by the coffin, painted with geometric motifs and bands of blue outlined in black, red, and white. The body was lying on its back. Fragments of a net of multicolored faience beads were found on the head and upper torso, suggesting the schematic representation of a human face. A pendant consisting of an unworked gold nugget was also found. Even more impressive was a set of seven vessels of hammered and polished bronze of approximately 85 percent copper and 15 percent tin. The hieroglyphic inscription chased on one of the vessels identifies the tomb as belonging to the *wab*-priest (*wab* or "pure" priests formed a lower class of priests) Penimen. The inscription consists of a dedicatory formula to the god Amun of Pnubs (the place-name Pnubs has long been associated with the sites of Kerma and Tabo). We now know, following recent discoveries, that this necropolis was associated with Dukki Gel. According to the evidence, this tomb may date to the Twenty-Fifth Dynasty or, more probably, to the early Napatan period.

The development of these vast necropolises is evidence of continuous occupation during several centuries, with gradual population growth until the Medieval period. The frequent shifts in the course of the Nile and its branches most certainly resulted in successive displacement of the cemeteries. Indeed, since prehistoric times, large burial grounds established on the edge of the Eastern Desert were displaced in stages, following the principal course of the river as it moved west. The main necropolis of ancient Kerma was located 4 kilometers from the cities along the Nile, but at the end of Classic Kerma a new cemetery was established closer to the city, near its port. It was the starting point for the many cemeteries located next to the urban areas.

A Royal Tomb

In the same area of the expanding modern city, 1 kilometer south of the Deffufa, we conducted a rescue excavation of an extraordinary structure over 6 meters deep dug into layers of clay and silt (Fig. 29). A homeowner, appalled by the presence of large stones from the neighboring cataract blocking her basement, requested that we remove these inconvenient remains. We were able to trace a masonry circle 17 meters in diameter on the surface. A wide staircase descended into this circular structure, projecting more than 4 meters toward the inside of the pit (Bonnet and Valbelle 2000, 144–156). The staircase was once surmounted by a chapel decorated with faience tiles, a type of structure entirely unknown before 1973. Clearing it required several seasons, especially since the fill was extremely compact and the lower levels penetrated the water table, requiring continuous pumping.

The strata were highly disturbed due to severe looting; the layers of sand, compacted silt, and soil were mixed with great quantities of fragmentary archaeological material. There is no doubt that this destruction was intentional. It was nevertheless possible to determine the richness of the objects, which included statue fragments, semiprecious stones, jewelry, and large quantities of gold leaf. Several faience slabs, especially on the steps of the staircase, had remnants of animal decoration. The ceramic material was quite diverse: caliciform red goblets with black rims (sometimes with an intermediary silver band), plates, shallow bowls, and large bowls. The presence of Egyptian wheel-made vessels provided the first indication of the transition from a long-lived Kerma tradition to initial Egyptian production, already evident in the final royal tombs of the eastern necropolis. Egyptian styles were already in abundance before the conquest by Thutmose I.

Large, roughly squared blocks were laid in irregular courses to form a funnel-shaped shaft. The wall was tightly packed against the alluvial soil by a filling of more irregular stones (Fig. 30). The wall was about 1 meter thick at the surface level, where collapsed fired bricks and mudbricks must have belonged to a sizable circular superstructure. A break in the wall made room for a staircase of thick slabs of ferruginous sandstone. There were two flights of

Fig. 29 The royal tomb during excavation

eleven steps each, separated by a landing. Despite extensive looting, a jar and traces of a hearth provide evidence that the deceased had not been entirely forgotten. A sheep appeared to have been sacrificed at the site of the tomb. Radiocarbon analysis provides a fairly early date for the hearth: circa 1400 BCE, after the end of Classic Kerma.

This royal tomb does not invite comparison with the most recent tumuli found in the eastern necropolis. It appears to signal a change in funerary customs, although the decoration of the chapel with its faience slabs closely resembled similar examples from the K XI and K II funerary temples. The ceramic material is identical with assemblages from the second half of Classic Kerma, and it seems certain that the burial is related to one of the last rulers of the kingdom, preceding the Egyptian conquest. It is most likely that the looting took place after the Pharaonic armies took control of the territory, after the apogee of the kingdom of Kerma, when its kings had been able to assert their power in the afterlife as well as in their earthly domain.

The burial areas of the C-Group also followed an evolution comparable to the funerary practices of Kerma (Fig. 31). Shortly before abandonment, larger tumuli with an adjoining chapel appeared in these cemeteries. Manfred Bietak, who studied the chronology of the C-Group occupation, believes that this land between Egypt and the kingdom of Kerma was probably subjected to intense Egyptian pressure at the end of Kerma's history (Bietak 1968). Starting with the beginning of the New Kingdom,

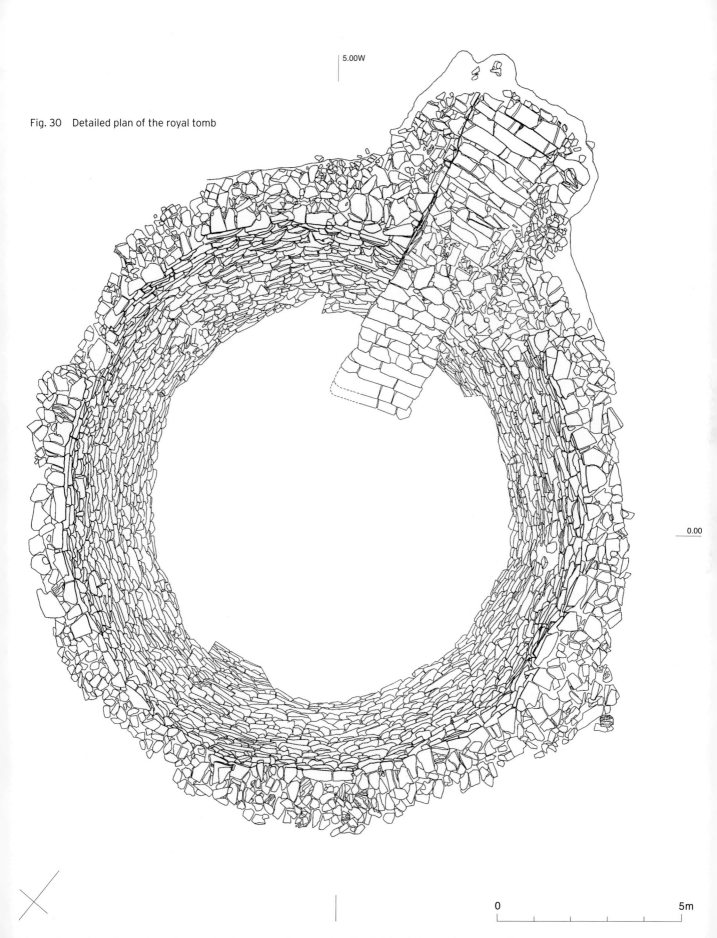

5.00W

Fig. 30   Detailed plan of the royal tomb

0.00

0   5m

Fig. 31   Reconstruction of the superstructure of the royal tomb

the orientations of graves and chapels were changed and mudbrick burial vaults were adopted—for example, in Dakka or the south of Aniba N. The position of the body is a chronological clue that also must be taken into account.

The royal tomb of Kerma has admittedly not yielded much information on its infrastructure, but a funerary chamber was probably erected on the pavement. The latter, located below the level of the water table, could only be observed in a very small area and under difficult conditions. Beyond the limits of the tomb itself, it was not possible to study the necropolis area. Lepsius reported at least two additional stone circles, so we can assume that the burial ground was quite large during Classic Kerma. Thus this rich discovery affirms once again the evolution of Nubian kingship. Comparison with C-Group cemeteries confirms a relationship between these two populations. For about a thousand years, the burials of these two lands were found alongside each other despite the rather clear separation of their territories.

PART II

Dukki Gel, an African City, and the *mnnw* of Thutmose I

The Site of Dukki Gel

It is unusual to discover two cities located so close to each other in ancient times (Fig. 32). For a considerable time we believed that a single urban site existed at Kerma—namely, the city that developed around the religious center of the Deffufa and its annexes. The Egyptian conquest precipitated the abandonment of the Nubian capital, while a new city was founded by Pharaoh Thutmose I at the neighboring site of Dukki Gel. From that moment on, colonization was the determining factor in the history of the region during the New Kingdom. The remains at Dukki Gel provide clear evidence of an Egyptian influence that should have led to the gradual disappearance of native features. Our first investigations at the site, however, have revealed that Egyptian occupation was followed by a native revival during the Twenty-Fifth Dynasty, when the Nubian kings gained control of their northern neighbors. Indeed, Pharaoh Taharqa went as far as to defend Egypt against Assyrian invaders (Bonnet 2015a, 19–26). After this episode, the Napatan kingdom unified Nubia once again, and the urban center of Dukki Gel resumed its importance as a regional metropolis. Still later, the city continued to grow under the

influence of the Meroitic Empire. Temples were reconstructed, giving the city a monumental aspect worthy of the ancient capital.

The first years of excavation at Dukki Gel aroused the expectation that certain native traditions had been preserved. It was obviously necessary to investigate later levels before excavating further in search of the earliest occupation. To do so took much patience since the mudbrick and *galous* construction required very careful scraping in order to understand the extensive rebuilding of foundations. We uncovered stratum after stratum in our effort to preserve as full a picture as possible of each phase over an extensive surface, dated by ceramics and inscribed or decorated architectural blocks.

It was quite a surprise to discover, near the eastern part of the site, an area with architecture noticeably different from that found in the ancient city of Kerma, as well as in the later Egyptian settlement at Dukki Gel (Bonnet 2012, 57–75). Equally striking was the density of the archaeological layers, as well as the fact that all the walls appeared to be curvilinear, resulting in circular or oval buildings (Fig. 33). The defensive systems were equally

Fig. 32   Aerial view of the archaeological sites of Kerma, Dukki Gel, and the port area (Google, 2016 Digital Globe)

impressive. The foundations, constantly modified, belonged to monuments that had no prototype along the entire length of the Nile Valley. By connecting some of the walls to the Egyptian religious complex of the Eighteenth Dynasty, we have determined that these singular buildings were earlier than or contemporary with the beginnings of the New Kingdom, a conclusion that is confirmed by the presence of sherds from the end of Classic Kerma (Fig. 34). We were thus in the presence of a city that predated the Egyptian conquest and prospered during the most flourishing period of the kingdom of Kerma.

Faced with this discovery, we may exclude the hypothesis that one city succeeded the other. We can only imagine that, during the long life of the kingdom of Kerma, a second urban complex

may have served a different population. This conjecture is fairly recent, as our excavations only reached the occupation levels in question eight years ago. Many years of additional research will be required to understand all the implications of this discovery, especially since the site extends beyond the excavated area. We are, however, in the presence of an immense indigenous site. Because it has been gradually encroached upon by farming (Bonnet 2015b, 1–14), we did not have free rein to extend the archaeological site; it was hardly possible to take over the neighboring properties, under cultivation by their owners for a very long time. We therefore searched for ways to preserve, as best we could, the most significant remains that had escaped destruction, while continuing to study the levels dating back to the origins of

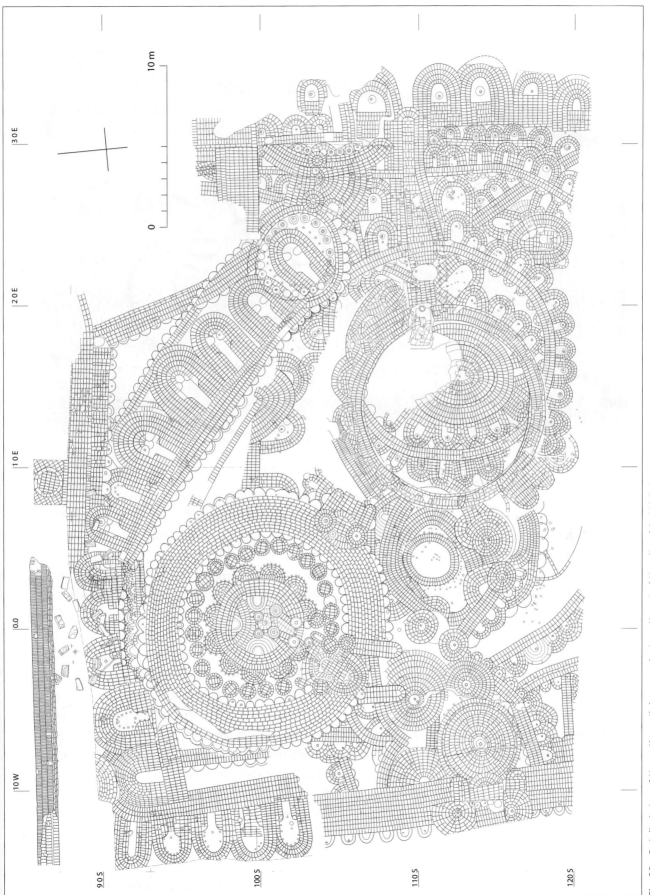

Fig. 33   Detailed plan of the native religious precinct northeast of the site of Dukki Gel

Fig. 34   The northeast religious precinct after restoration

what we consider to be a site connected to central Africa.

This preliminary work has revealed a singular architectural style that prevailed during a fairly ancient period. Given the current state of excavation, it is not possible to state with certainty that the buildings uncovered to date belonged to a central Sudanese population, although we do believe this to be the case. Indeed, our trenches are not deep enough to allow the recovery of associated archaeological material. As a precaution, we made a concerted effort to follow a horizontal stratigraphy before uncovering earlier levels. Nevertheless, urbanization and building type have provided comparative data: this style of architecture is related to a known African tradition, though only relatively late models of the nineteenth and twentieth centuries survive. In reviewing ancient Egyptian texts concerning warfare with enemies to the south, we learn that the pharaonic armies confronted coalitions. It is thus possible to consider the existence of a federation of sorts created at the initiative of the king of Kerma to maximize the strength of his forces. Dukki Gel may have functioned as an indispensable ceremonial and military center that accommodated the armies of the southern kingdoms. Troop encampments have not yet been identified, but recent geomagnetic survey has yielded a preliminary image of installations that subsequent excavation should clarify (Bonnet 2017).

The Ceremonial City of Dukki Gel

Around the Egyptian cult monuments and palaces discovered during the past twenty years, we excavated archaeological levels that had not been covered by later construction and had probably been subjected to wind erosion, as indicated by ceramic material abandoned since Napatan times. We also observed changes in topography following a climatic phase that occurred during the beginning of the Napatan period, when accumulations of sand formed actual dunes in some locations. During the centuries from the end of the New Kingdom to the Twenty-Fifth Dynasty, occupational levels were profoundly disturbed. We were not always able to follow the stages of urban development, as they were often obscured by heaps of sand several meters high. Despite these difficulties, we have established a solid chronology for the Egyptian buildings and their fortifications and are able, as a result, to identify building activity following the conquest by Thutmose I and the successive phases of construction. As far as preceding levels are concerned, for the moment we can reconstruct them only partially. Our results are therefore preliminary and their interpretation will evolve with future investigation.

Now, however, we can propose a preliminary picture of the African city after reconstructing the plans of the principal buildings uncovered in full or with sondages (Fig. 35). Several segments of the internal enclosure wall have allowed us to define an urban core measuring 170 by 80 meters. The northern section of the wall, 6 meters thick, was collapsed at the east and west corners, unlike the southern side. What is striking, upon examining the general plan, is the presence of numerous gates each incorporating two towers, thus creating relatively narrow doorways. These towers were constructed in concentric courses of mudbrick; the best-preserved masonry is ten courses high. The foundations of the largest towers, up to 14 meters in diameter, are anchored by a system of rounded and hardened clods of earth that served as bases for square vertical beams. These clods, whose diameter varies from 0.45 to 0.60 meters, were encircled by a peripheral mudbrick wall 1 meter thick. Sometimes there was also an arrangement of aligned supporting elements, probably indicating the location of a stairway to an upper wooden platform for use by the guards.

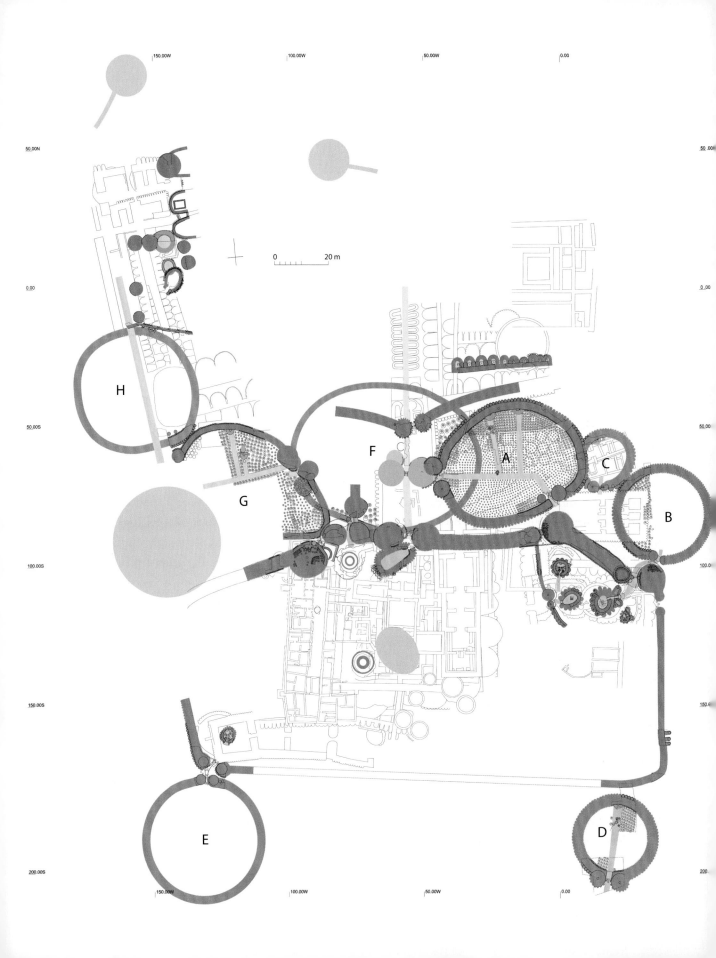

150.00W   100.00W   50.00W   0.00

50.00N   50.00

0.00   0.00

0   20 m

H

50.00S   50.00

A
F   C
G   B

100.00S   100.0

150.00S   150.0

E   D

200.00S   200.

150.00W   100.00W   50.00W   0.00

Fig. 35   Schematic plan of Dukki Gel circa 1600–1500 BCE

Thus we have evidence for an architectural style whose building techniques sprang from a tradition other than Nubian or Egyptian, especially given the great deal of diversity in construction details. The layout of the wooden and earth supports can vary, forming, for example, a narrower ring that affects the thickness of the facings. The two entrance towers of the same door were generally of varying diameter, with walls often supported by small and regular buttresses extending along the enclosure wall. Wooden doors usually had two leaves. Their position can be reconstructed from pivot holes and a central closing mechanism. These different features, all rounded in shape, were made of an extraordinarily resistant silt; on their surface are traces of wear caused by the movement of the door leaf. As for the central accommodation for the closing mechanism, a square stake impression is still visible in the hardened silt. The threshold usually consisted of a rectilinear base in brick.

Protected by its enclosure, the city must have been densely populated, although later building activity has obliterated the oldest traces of occupation. Two wells, constructed with considerable effort, may

have motivated, at least in part, the foundation of the settlement. The well to the north was dug into a pit of considerable width. The peripheral wall was constructed of *galous,* with a step outward 2 meters from the bottom and a second step slightly higher to widen the circular opening even more. This peripheral wall was interrupted on the west to make room for a staircase or ramp descending to water level and facilitating circulation while drawing water (Fig. 36). The well was supported by a structure of stone blocks and accessed through one of the double-towered city gates. It is interesting to note that the east tower was associated with yet a third tower, with which it formed another gate. This entrance, relatively narrow, may have been reserved for specific ceremonies, as was the case later during the Meroitic Period (Marchi 2017). The gate opened onto a kind of terrace that today is eroded; it has been truncated and no longer leads to the lower level and the water. The gate was of modest proportions when compared with its much used and constantly altered neighbor, located at the foot of one of the largest towers of the city. The central well, also with *galous* walls, was frequently remodeled during

Fig. 36   The north well in 2015

the New Kingdom, at which time it was associated with two temples (Fig. 37). The well water must have been considered sacred from the very beginning, but we have no evidence for the original structure that enclosed it. Ceramic material dating to Classic Kerma was recovered from the upper levels of the well.

In the middle of the area near the central well, we discovered numerous tuyere fragments of impressive size, measuring 0.80 meters in length. The diameter of the smaller end measured 10 to 12 centimeters; the larger end, 30 to 40 centimeters. As several of these tuyeres were recovered, we can assume that a bronze furnace existed on the site of what was to become, in the Eighteenth Dynasty, the central temple of Dukki Gel. In the religious precinct west of the Deffufa at Kerma, we also discovered the remains of a furnace, affirming the presence of a

bronze workshop in the Nubian capital as early as Middle Kerma. It is therefore hardly surprising to find a major workshop in the neighboring city, most probably next to a cult installation destroyed by later Egyptian construction. The techniques involved in the casting of metal were complex and testify to the skill of the native population.

Located along the central axis of the city, the entryway of the monumental gate was often modified, either in dimensions or in orientation. In a final stage, the threshold and pivot holes were shifted to the east. This gate gave directly onto the opening of a long building measuring 10 by 4 meters internally. Buttresses reinforced the exceptionally thick walls; we can assume that the building was vaulted. Renovations carried out on the buttresses indicate a fairly long period of use. In comparison with other monuments located farther to the east, we

Fig. 37   Aerial view of the remains of three Egyptian temples at Dukki Gel

can interpret this building as a cult installation. It suffered greatly due to construction work because of its location near the entrance to the main Egyptian temple and other, later temples. Several postholes may also be associated with a later occupation, as yet poorly understood.

The northeast corner of the city was separated by a modest enclosure wall flanked by small connected bastions. Two monumental gates opened through the main wall of the urban complex, and a side entrance provided secondary access to the outside (Fig. 35). Inside the city walls, a small gate with two towers, 4 and 2 meters in diameter, led to the center. The most important building in the separate area was a fairly small oval chamber (4.50 by 3.75 meters) inside a thick wall supported by large rounded bastions, anchored in the soil by stakes (Bonnet 2009, 98–108). This arrangement suggests

a vaulted ceiling that required strong buttressing. The chamber, paved in brick, had postholes in its center, probably delimiting a naos. The entrance, on the east side, was through a long corridor protected by two V-shaped bastions (Bonnet 2011b, 7–9). During the New Kingdom, this corridor widened as it joined a defensive system, but it was originally a shorter passage bordered by a double fence of wooden posts and, probably, interlacing branches, leading to one of the monumental gates.

The path outside the gate, evident from its well-trodden surface, rounded the large tower and turned at right angles toward the door of a vast colonnaded building that we have interpreted as a palace (B) (Bonnet 2013, 810–812) (Fig. 38). This oval structure with its system of vaults may have been connected to a cult, as it was maintained on the same spot until the end of the Meroitic period—in other

words, for 2,000 years. It underwent multiple transformations and, under the Napatan kingdom, was provided with a wooden naos adorned with a bronze cornice encrusted with small plaques of lapis lazuli and gold leaf. This association of two monuments leads us to conclude that the Egyptian model of ceremonial palace and temple may have played a role at Dukki Gel, especially since several palaces of impressive proportions have been found in the city, and it is certain that other religious buildings existed as well.

The location of the naos can be reconstructed from postholes in the pattern of a circular structure, analogous to the dome-shaped structure in stone from Gebel Barkal. The arrangement of the chapels erected at a later date on either side of the entrance corridor provides other examples. Each chapel was a scaled-down version of a cult installation—small oval chamber and vault supported by a robust wall—and featured, on the south side, two steps leading up to a rectangular brick pedestal. A naos may have existed here as well. The same arrangement was found in a second, and later, religious structure a bit farther west in the same cult precinct. It, too, was oval in shape, with a vaulted central chamber supported by a buttressed wall. Several building phases were identified in the central space. The first consisted of a low rounded wall around a rectangular pedestal preceded by a staircase, oriented north-south, as in the other examples just mentioned. Next, a second low oval wall was added around the original one, probably to hide or protect the naos. Still later, a double row of posts either consolidated the second low wall or provided a double barrier. Two circular jambs, restored several times, supported the door of this cult building. Slightly farther north, a circular building was

Fig. 38   Two doorways of Palace B

uncovered in contemporaneous levels. Its cramped interior was restricted by a thick wall supported by semicircular bastions, shorter in length than was usual in cult structures. The entrance, with doorjambs consisting of columns of bricks, opened to the south, toward the western cult area. The slightly off-center alignment of the doorway made it impossible to see the far end of the room. The center of the chamber contained a square baldachin with four columns surrounding a circular offering table with small earth decorations around its perimeter. On the same axis, three steps led up to a seat against the north wall. Two additional seats were located on either side.

This spatial arrangement shows similarities with the chamber at the far end of the Egyptian ceremonial palaces. It is therefore possible that the native religious precinct included, in a period contemporary with the Kerma cultures, a circular palace inside the city wall. It was soon enlarged with an enormous peripheral wall 17 meters in diameter. The inside wall was crowned with a row of columns, and a wide doorway opened onto a monumental passage leading to the place of worship. A few rare Classic Kerma sherds establish the chronology of this reli-

gious precinct at the beginning of the New Kingdom. The second cult precinct was thus associated with a palace protected by the city walls. When it was reconstructed, this palace was furnished with a second door opening toward the main temple. Palace B, located outside the walls, may have been abandoned during a period of conflict in favor of the protected religious precinct and its palace.

In fact, this protective arrangement was only increased during subsequent periods. After the Egyptian conquest, complex defensive systems were erected, although the invaders continued to maintain the native places of worship in the fortress. Inside the southwest corner of the city wall, we investigated the remains of another palace (Fig. 39). Oval in shape, it was oriented north-south with its entrance to the south. A thick wall supported by semicircular buttresses enclosed a chamber 14 meters in length. In the center was an offering table of hardened silt under a baldachin suggested by four columns. On the north side, a large rounded staircase led to an earthen throne built against the wall. Two benches against the wall on either side of the throne completed the arrangement. Next to this

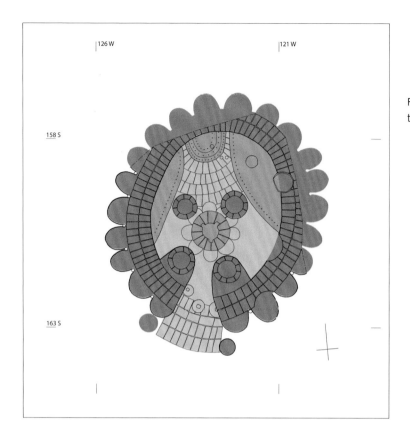

Fig. 39 A small native palace to the southwest

small palace, topographical evidence suggests the presence of a second building, yet to be excavated. It may have housed a cult.

The southwest corner of the enclosure is partially preserved, with an entry flanked by two towers more than 4 meters in diameter. The gateway, 2 meters wide, was altered several times; it gave onto the door of a large palace (E) extending to the south. Several sondages revealed numerous rows of mudbrick columns very close to one another. Palace E was at least 44 meters in diameter. It probably bordered a ceremonial way that connected the two cities of Kerma and Dukki Gel, passing through fortification systems that blocked the route. The corner of the city fortification wall, probably leveled during the wars at the beginning of the New Kingdom, was replaced by a rounded building whose plan, although irregular, was presumably circular originally. On the inside, a hundred or so columns, relatively spaced out, supported a lightweight roof. We are left with the

impression that this building had taken the place of a gate and was possibly used as an entry vestibule.

On the other side of the city, in the southeast, the enclosure wall was identified by limited sondages only. Here the city was protected by connected bastions whose layout does not appear to be systematic. While an entrance gate into the city remains hypothetical, geomagnetic survey has identified substantial remains on the western side of a circular building that functioned as a palace. From the door on the south side of the building, a paved aisle led to a throne. A baldachin surmounting an offering table was located several meters in front of the throne. Nearby, low walls were linked to a door-closing system. Throughout the building, column bases were preserved, so closely spaced that they impeded traffic.

Our understanding of this ceremonial center is partial at best, as we lack the foundations of the most important cult buildings. Since the original protected area was continuously occupied for centuries, earlier structures have suffered as a result. Furthermore, the presence of the Kom of the Bodegas, a mound almost 8 meters high composed of fragments of Napatan and Meroitic bread molds that were discarded after baking, covers a major sector of the city. According to the geomagnetic evidence, an elongated gateway may have provided access to this area. It was simply not possible to remove this mound, so characteristic of the site, that gives it its name: Dukki Gel means "red mound" in the Nubian language. Other areas that we may study in the coming years will allow us to verify the functions of the buildings in the urban center that would appear, above all, to have met ceremonial needs. We have indirect proof for this hypothesis all around this area, where several palaces have already been excavated.

Along the northern enclosure wall, Palace A offers a good example of this African style of architecture (Fig. 40). Oval in plan, the palace measures 58 by 45 meters (Bonnet 2013, 811–817). Its peripheral wall was very thick and reinforced in places by small, semicircular, connected buttresses. Two doors provided access, one from the west and one from the south. They were linked by a paved aisle

from which two more perpendicular aisles, also paved, branched off. Each side aisle led to a throne against the north wall of the building. In front of the west throne, an offering table protected by a low wall was encircled by the column bases of a baldachin. As many as 1,400 columns of small diameter supported a roof of wood and palm fibers or reeds. Probably to ensure the stability of the structure, the foundation of each column was more than a meter deep. This plan is unique (Fig. 41), without equivalent in any Egyptian or Nubian palace. At present, it can only be compared to central African structures of centuries past.

How should we interpret this extraordinary number of mudbrick columns? They were very tightly spaced and, apart from the aisles leading to the thrones, made it almost impossible to move about in the building. A preliminary answer may be proposed upon considering the site of Kasubi, on one of the hills of Kampala in Uganda (Moriset et al. 2011). The last rulers of the kingdom of Buganda were interred at this site. Admittedly, several millennia separate it from the palace of Dukki Gel, but the cult precinct of Kasubi is also the location of an

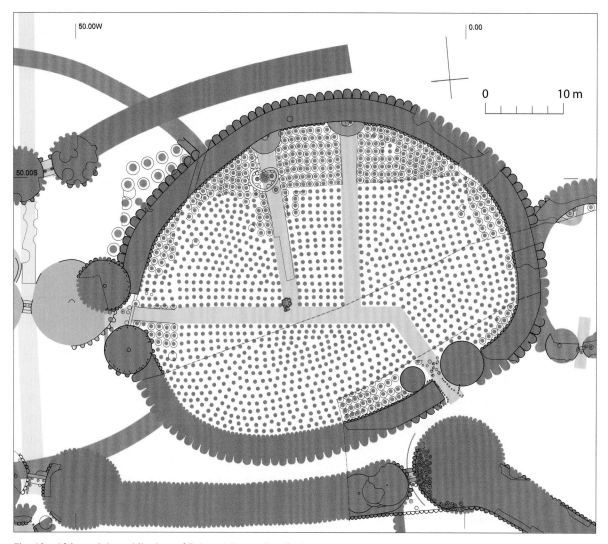

Fig. 40   African-style architecture of Palace A (reconstruction)

ancient African palace visited by the explorer Henry Stanley in 1875. The palace is constructed of wood, with a roof thatched with bundles of straw. Curtains of bark isolate a large portion of the room from the "sacred forest" or *kibira*. The entrance hut to the palace leads into the first courtyard, which contains numerous circular constructions. Temples, palaces, and funerary areas, located side by side, may represent features of a complex tradition that considerably predates the Middle Ages.

Another ceremonial palace (G) is currently under study in the northwest area of Dukki Gel. Ovoid in plan, it measured more than 60 meters in length. An aisle leading to several thrones ran across the interior. An enclosure next to one of the thrones may have housed a cult installation with a square altar pedestal surmounted by a baldachin. Large offering tables, occasionally rebuilt, were associated with the various thrones. Two entrances, each flanked by two towers, opened through the rather narrow building

Fig. 41   Palace A and later structures, after restoration

wall, about 2 meters thick. A sondage in the eastern part of Palace G revealed an earlier phase 0.80 meters below the current structure. Several building phases in succession remain to be excavated, comparable to Palace C, whose remains are covered by Palaces A and B.

In line with the main entrance, in the center of the north side of the ceremonial city, the remains of several gates were found. Each consisted of two towers that are more or less aligned, an orientation later followed by the dromos after the Egyptian conquest. A brick-paved alley also followed the same line, preserved for a length of 10 meters or so. Sixty meters away from the enclosure wall, beneath Egyptian fortifications of the New Kingdom, a stretch of defensive wall with connected bastions suggests the location of a second enclosure, also part of the fortifications of the original city. The plan of this defensive structure is still quite fragmentary; it appears to have belonged to a complex system with hybrid structures that remains to be studied. Moreover, the picture we have of its west side, with circular bastions, is quite different.

What really distinguishes the main gate is an immense oval structure (F), measuring almost 70 by 64 meters (Fig. 35). With larger, more widely spaced columns, it is quite different from the palaces uncovered around the exterior of the ceremonial city. Building F, which predates the fortress of Thutmose I, is partially covered by the foundations of Palaces A and G. The northern gate of the fortress apparently impinged on part of Building F and probably replaced it. The building was probably closer in function to a gatehouse or entrance hut, similar to the example cited above from Kasubi in Uganda. Called a *bujjabukula,* this type of structure is well known in central Africa, where it is often located next to an altar or a sacred tree. This entrance hut was a place where people could easily assemble to await an audience.

Egyptian architects rebuilt the entrance to the ceremonial city. Instead of an oval columned building, they constructed a fortified gate, along with an imposing hypostyle hall that cut through Building F, which was leveled as far as the entrance to the central temple of Thutmose I. The oval architectural plan was replaced by an orthogonal design with an inside passage, the monumentality of the new plan overwhelming the earlier colonnaded hall. To increase its impact, a foregate was constructed in front of the fortified entry, echoing the native architectural plan, which tended to stress a prominent feature easily visible in front of the city's defenses. This external feature served not only to emphasize an important entry but also to remind people of the location of a place of worship or, possibly, a building essential to the very survival of the city.

During our most recent excavation season, a second axis, emphasized by a gigantic gate with a foregate, was uncovered. Once again, an enormous building (H) appears to have been designed to serve as a vestibule one had to pass through before entering the city (Fig. 56). The two excavated stretches of wall do not permit a full reconstruction of a circular plan at least 46 meters in diameter. The few columns uncovered are widely spaced and the peripheral wall, 3 to 4 meters thick, is formidable. Building H was probably protected by a bastioned enclosure that we were able to trace on the northeast side. The central axis across the building continued southward as a road flanked by low walls, in the direction of a large circular monument. The latter building was located just outside the city wall, between the two fortification systems. An initial sondage revealed bastions around a central plan. By comparison with similar structures, this building may have served as a native cult installation, but additional excavation is necessary to confirm this hypothesis.

Entry vestibule H was not an isolated building; on the contrary, it appears to have been surrounded by multiple constructions, suggesting military and religious functions. The passage that crossed building H continued to the north where, 70 meters on, we cleared a series of large circular structures that may have belonged to a fortification line continuing beyond the area of excavation. Other structures, not fully studied, were located on the east side. The ends of three bastions may define fortification works 40 meters long, but it is not possible at this time to compare them to other defensive structures at Dukki Gel. Their internal features included a stairway leading up to a walkway, probably protected behind merlons. This massive defensive system faces the north-south axis and must be quite old, if sherds of Classic Kerma are any indication.

Other oval or circular installations approximately 10 meters in diameter belonged to military structures with internal features leading to upper platforms. Narrow doorways on the lower level were associated with stairs. The good state of preservation of the mud-brick masonry made it easier to understand the superimpositions resulting from multiple refurbishing of the defenses. At present it is difficult to follow the general layout of this limited area. To extend our field of vision, we called upon two geomagnetic specialists, Tomasz M. Herbich and Robert S. Ryndziewicz, to conduct an underground survey near the northwest gate as well as in a field south of the concession of Dukki Gel. It was essential to determine whether these areas were connected to Nubian, Egyptian, or African architectural traditions. We also hoped to recover chronological information.

The results of the resistivity survey surpassed our highest expectations, revealing an extraordinary ensemble with circular constructions covering almost

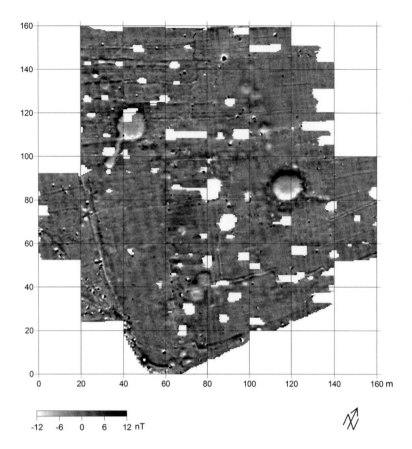

Fig. 42 Plan of geomagnetic survey conducted by Tomasz Herbich and Robert Ryndziewicz; blank spaces indicate palm trees

the entire area (Fig. 42). The structures identified range from 1 or 2 up to 15 or 20 meters in diameter. Two substantial monuments are quite distinct; both are lined with bastions and are comparable to a cult installation uncovered in the northeast quarter of the urban center (Fig. 43). A long fortified corridor led to the entry of each building. The narrow entry passages were oriented according to the principal roads leading to the main gates. This comparison confirms that cult installations were located before the gates of the ceremonial city, and also that the urban complex gradually grew to occupy a considerable area.

This city, African in character, represents an architectural style without known parallel. Also noteworthy is the fact that it dates to a historical period, which further excavation should allow us to date more precisely. Second, while the religious and mili-

tary functions of the city have been well established, domestic structures with contemporaneous archaeological material remain to be discovered. Indeed, the ceramics and few rare objects recovered belong to Nubia and Egypt, while the structures themselves reflect the traditions of more southerly populations and should have been accompanied by examples of central African material culture. Admittedly, the superimposition of occupation levels hardly facilitates interpretation, especially since mudbrick architecture leaves behind complicated remains of minimal height. Foundations are crushed and even the most careful excavation disturbs each phase. The fact that architecture was originally rounded, followed by quadrangular, helps to distinguish the phases, especially since Nubian buildings are rare at Dukki Gel in this period of the early New Kingdom.

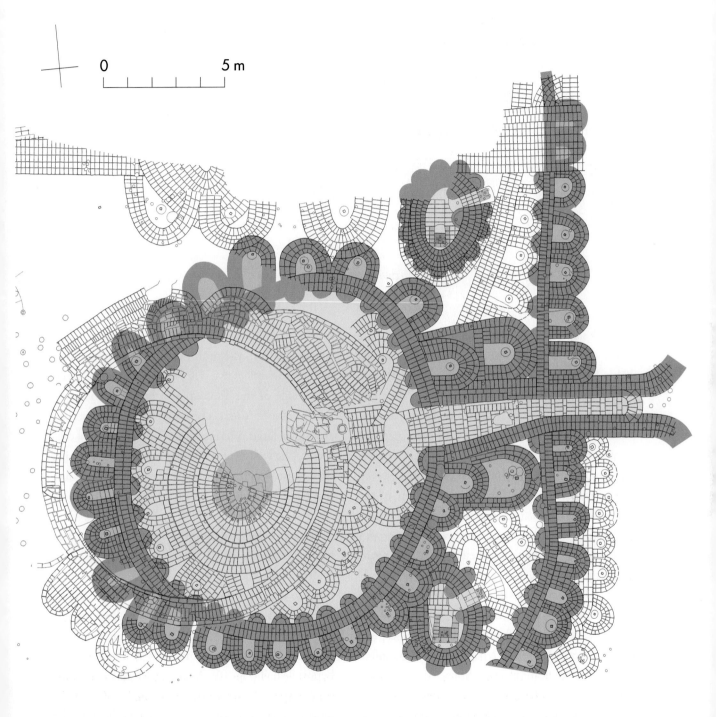

Fig. 43 Detailed plan of the main cult precinct in the northeast; native construction under Hatshepsut

A Later Intervention in Palace A

We have seen that it is still difficult to determine the phases of transformation of the African city (Bonnet 2013, 814–816). Certainly, several gates with two towers each were located along the axis of the main entry (Fig. 44). The two phases of Palace G have been partially revealed. As for the large gateway towers of the urban center, they bear evidence of several rebuilding phases. One of the small towers was even shifted 4 meters during an alteration of the gateway. The work carried out on the gate of the central axis is even more significant because the towers were dug out again, giving their foundations an irregular plan. Here, too, the gateway was slightly shifted. These structures did not escape the problems posed by the upkeep of mudbrick masonry, as was also the case for the residences of the Nubian capital: walls were under constant repair, a process that often resulted in significant modifications.

The west side of Palace A was completely reconstructed. While we do not know if the previous palace was torn down, it is clear that the west entry was revamped because the north tower was partially removed from the outside to make room for a chapel at right angles to the doorway (Fig. 45). A solid wall closed off the west side of the chapel. Entrance was from the south, through a porch ending in a semicircle; two internal columns flanked either side of the door. Inside the small chamber, the four bases for a canopy support were preserved around a large offering table 1.40 meters in diameter. The walls were probably covered with a thick whitewash, fragments of which were scattered over the table and floor. Despite these modifications, the door of Palace A was still in use, as evidenced by a paved passage that followed the transverse course of the previous path.

Turning to the left upon entering Palace A, it was possible to reach a narrow passage between two massive circular structures hiding a door. Beyond this feature, a façade consisting of two elongated bastions framed an entrance opening into a 13-meter-long hypostyle hall (Fig. 46). A double row of five massive columns must have created quite an impression. A series of small buttresses emphasized the bases of the columns. The very regular side walls met the back wall where a throne, preceded by three steps, rested against the wall. This throne room may have replaced a previous one, but this architectural ensemble, which

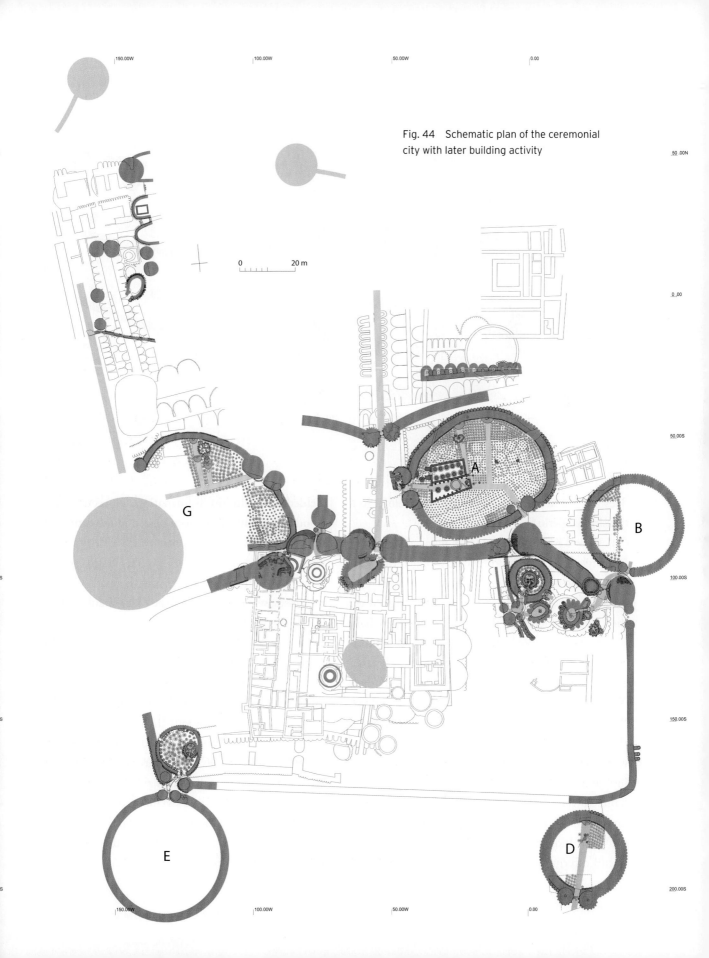

Fig. 44   Schematic plan of the ceremonial
city with later building activity

150.00W   100.00W   50.00W   0.00

50.00N

0.00

50.00S

100.00S

150.00S

200.00S

0   20 m

G

A

B

E

D

150.00W   100.00W   50.00W   0.00

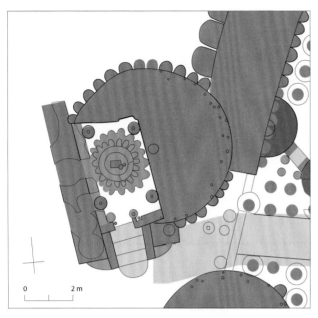

Fig. 45   Native chapel constructed inside the entry tower of Palace A

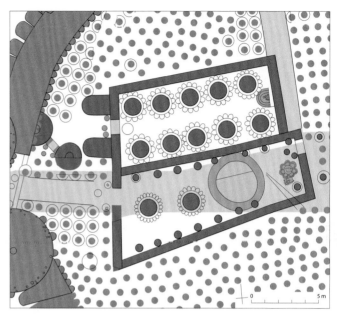

Fig. 46   Throne room and libation basin in Palace A

does not follow the African norms, may belong to a transitional period.

A second room, trapezoidal in plan, adjoined the hypostyle hall to the south. Slightly longer, the walls of the room were supported by a series of small columns along the interior. Two columns aligned on the long axis, identical to those in the hypostyle hall, supported a lightweight roof. An aisle paved in mud-brick led along one side of the room to a fairly large circular basin where footprints were preserved, then continued eastward past an offering table to a door. Worshippers probably stopped at the basin, leaving their prints in damp soil opposite a tree or bush whose roots were in the bottom of the basin. The jujube immediately springs to mind; as it gave its name to the city of Pnubs, the tree was certainly known in this period. A water discharge duct behind the basin indicates an abundant use of water. The round offering table encircled by small buttresses

yielded a wealth of information. A rectangular wooden box must have been placed in the center of the table; excavated in its entirety, it yielded Classic Kerma sherds, including tulip beaker fragments. A rectangular offering table, also with small pointed buttresses, was added against the older circular table. Both were handmade of clay.

The discovery of an African city more than 1,000 kilometers north of Central Sudan is, in itself, an enigma for further archaeological investigation to solve (Fig. 47). In the current state of research, we know almost nothing about the occupation of the immense territory of the Sahel during the second and third millennia BCE. Excavations conducted by the Italian mission to Kassala have revealed the existence of a complex state (Manzo 2012, 75–106); it is also worth mentioning the Land of Punt, which probably joined the coalitions against the pharaonic armies. The remains observed by A. J. Arkell in

Fig. 47   General view of the archaeological site of Dukki Gel, with the northwest foregate in the foreground

Darfur also provide indirect evidence for the long history of this region (Arkell 1961; 1951–1952). The traditional forty-day route to Kordofan and Darfur is still today part of a trade network (Gratien et al. 2013) that bestowed upon Kerma its role as a crossroads. It is not unreasonable to think that this kingdom, independent from Egypt, was able to expand its power with the help of populations far-ther south. For its part, Egypt, which had sought since the Middle Kingdom to control the trade in essential products, would increasingly interfere by sending armies; for a long time, however, these efforts were ineffectual. Colonization did not occur until the New Kingdom. Archaeological studies are opening new avenues of thought into the circumstances of these upheavals.

The Egyptian Conquest of Nubia

Pharaoh Thutmose I occupied the ceremonial city upon his conquest of Nubia. Egyptian armies systematically destroyed the large African buildings in order to establish a *mnnw*: an institution in enemy territory that included religious and palatial buildings as well as food reserves (Somaglino 2010). The settlement was strongly fortified to protect tribute collected from the local population and maintain control over conquered territory. Since the ambitious building program implemented by Egypt required local labor, there is no doubt that the Egyptian forces reached a compromise with their Nubian subjects. At the initiative of Thutmose I, a true city was established, very far from Thebes, with a complex of several grandiose monuments constructed of mudbrick as the main building material. We may, indeed, ask ourselves if certain architectural choices were not influenced by the building methods of the Nubian overseers.

Archaeological exploration has been conducted over the course of some twenty years as, going back in time from the end of the Meroitic period, we have tried to understand successive occupation levels. Mudbrick remains, although well preserved, have undergone successive building phases, which, fortunately, could be analyzed thanks to the relative chronology. More than 1,000 inscribed or decorated architectural blocks bearing the cartouches of several kings helped in dating. These blocks are, sad to say, very fragmentary, but the painstaking work of Dominique Valbelle has yielded a rich harvest of information (Valbelle 2005a, 33–50; 2008, 85–93). The temples certainly benefited from the constant exertions of the magistrates overseeing them, as the great rulers of the Eighteenth Dynasty wanted to demonstrate their control over the region with prestigious buildings.

The chronology of the site also relies on ceramic studies, Nubian (Privati 1999, 41–69; 2004, 145–146) as much as Egyptian (Ruffieux 2005, 255–263; 2009, 121–134). The appearance of wheel-made pottery, influenced by Egyptian examples of buff-colored ware, provides a useful point of reference. This characteristic material has yielded a fairly clear sequence, and recent progress has allowed us to refine dating. The question whether this pottery was imported was solved once a vast workshop was discovered in the *mnnw* of Thutmose I; the sherds inventoried on-site indicate that local production continued for a long time during the New Kingdom.

The succession of temples and other monuments was thus established after a detailed analysis of archaeological layers. We were also able to determine that, at the end of the reign of Thutmose I, a Nubian coalition returned to power and the structures of the *mnnw* were almost entirely dismantled. With native forces in charge of a new architectural program, defensive works were undertaken throughout the site. The fortification walls of this transitional period indicate the resumption of central African influence. While the duration of this reorganization phase remains unclear, the return of the Egyptians during the reigns of Thutmose II and especially Hatshepsut is particularly well attested (Gabolde 2004, 129–148). The rebuilding of the *mnnw* is most impressive, as the Egyptian rulers, in response to the fortification works and recent achievements of the native population, expended considerable effort. Wishing to restore the grandeur of the city as it had been under their father, they reconstructed buildings along more generous proportions, using stone for certain privileged structures while maintaining the plan of the former *mnnw,* still recognizable despite destruction (Valbelle 2013, 447–464).

The *mnnw* of Thutmose I

The general plan of the *mnnw* established by Thutmose I is a concrete manifestation of an institution well known from texts but seldom found in the archaeological record (Fig. 48). The Aswan stela mentions several *mnnw* established by Thutmose I in this region, and the violent reaction of his son Thutmose II when he learned of the destruction inflicted by three rebellious war chieftains is ample evidence of the conflict that affected the city of Pnubs (Gabolde 2004, 129–148). Data gathered in the field have helped us understand the scale of the institutional program carried out by the Egyptians after they razed the ceremonial city and its first enclosure wall. Three temples would occupy the center of the city, probably replacing native places of worship. Two existing wells certainly helped determine the location of the three temples.

FORTIFICATIONS

The main temple was reached through the gate in the northern fortification wall, a truly imposing structure that obliterated the previous African-style installation (F). The Egyptian gate had two double bastions placed one behind the other, framing a doorway whose axis continued for a considerable distance to both north and south (Fig. 49). Two side corridors also provided access to the *mnnw*. In front of this gate was a foregate several dozen meters long, also with three parallel corridors. This foregate, which projected well beyond the fortifications, was the solution Egyptian architects chose to replace African-style entry vestibules (Bonnet 2015b, 2).

A thick wall supported by small buttresses ran along the outside of the long, rectangular mass of fortifications. On the inside, the three corridors were defended by connected bastions facing outward, reached from the central passage (Fig. 50). Cross corridors linked the three passages and facilitated the flow of traffic. The corridor in front of the north bastions of the gate could be closed off in several places, as evidenced by pivot holes and central fastening devices. These corridors were used by soldiers to scale the bastions (which were several meters high) to defend the gate. To maintain the rectilinear alignment and height of the ensemble, each bastion was constructed around a central circular support; the bastions of the foregate contained two, perhaps to strengthen their cohesion.

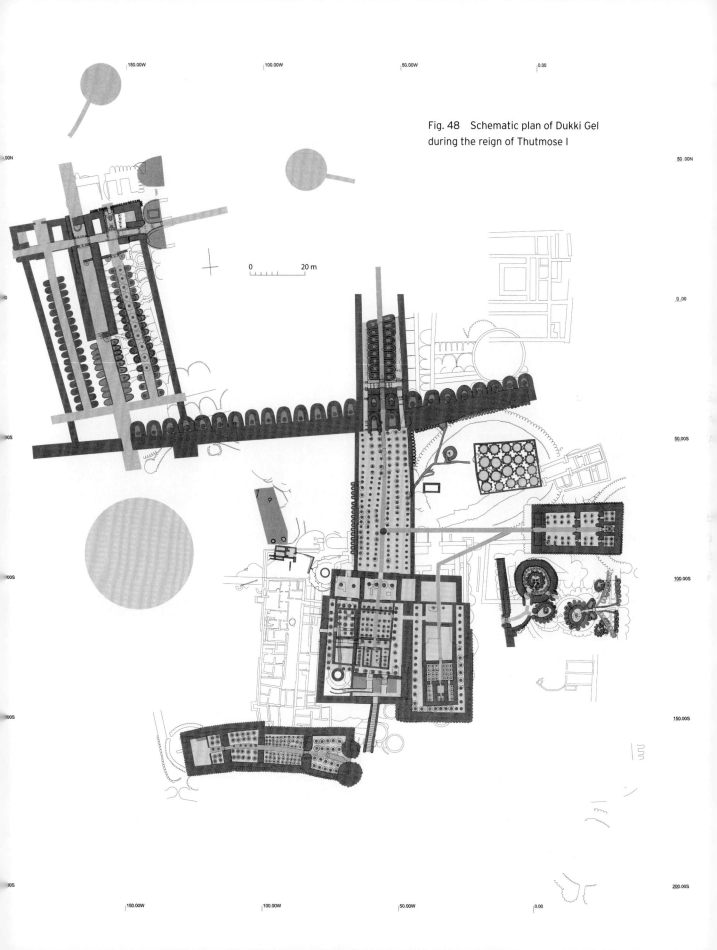

Fig. 48   Schematic plan of Dukki Gel
during the reign of Thutmose I

0   20 m

Fig. 49   Detailed plan of the north gate of the *mnnw* of Thutmose I

Fig. 50   Aerial view of the north gate and the large hypostyle entrance hall during the reign of Thutmose I, after restoration

On the lower level, the corridors were blocked by numerous double-shuttered closures, arranged along the gate or along the axis. They were rebuilt or shifted according to military needs. The four enormous bastions of the gate must have towered above the defensive complex as a whole, adding to the monumental appearance of the gate. Even so, a platform surmounted by the massive bastions must have existed 3 or 4 meters above the corridors. Stairways have not been preserved in the lower levels of the building, but we can conclude that the various landings must have been easily accessible (Fig. 51). Egyptian fortresses of the Second Cataract offer multiple comparisons to help us understand the defensive systems conceived at Dukki Gel. The formidable barrier established on the granitic bedrock of the Belly of Rocks dates to the Middle Kingdom, but later works cannot be dated with any precision. At Buhen, the projecting gate of the external enclosure, with its

monumental foregate, belonged to a later phase. Although the presence of an elaborate foregate was not a regular feature, it did at least exist. Such was the case at Mirgissa, where foregates projected onto the slope down to the Nile. Beginning in the Middle Kingdom, Egyptian architects designed fortified gates that were meant to overawe the beholder. As for the double bastions of the Dukki Gel gate, they have parallels at Kor, near Buhen, where the north and south gates were protected by two parallel bastions (Smith 1966, 187–232). But there again, this layout postdated the Middle Kingdom. At Mirgissa, the partially excavated outer wall also had a gate with two bastions (Vercoutter 1965, 62–64), comparable to the gates of Kerma, where this layout was in use by the end of Early Kerma. But the two rows of double bastions protecting the north gate of Dukki Gel, as conceived by the architects of Thutmose I, were an innovation.

Fig. 51   Reconstruction of the north gate and foregate complex under Thutmose I

Parts of the enclosure wall were removed on either side of the gate, which was flanked by attached semicircular bastions, unknown in Egypt or at the Second Cataract. The wall was 6 to 8 meters thick. Defensive bastions 6 meters long were arranged around masonry reinforcement 2 meters in diameter located at the entrance of the complex. The inside of the enclosure wall was reinforced with small rounded buttresses. They were interrupted just before the entrance to make room for a hydraulic installation. Rainwater flowing from the tops of the enclosure walls was probably collected by means of a vertical channel. A circular basin below the channel provided a drinking trough for cattle; hundreds of hoofprints were found in and around the basin, and along a wide channel with sloping sides lined with mudbrick.

This fortified northern front was superimposed over the exterior walls of palaces A and G, and also destroyed part of the wall of vestibule F. We picked up the line of fortification more than 50 meters to the west, where a second monumental foregate was aligned north-south at a slightly oblique angle to the enclosure of Thutmose I. Although part of this gate is still covered by later remains, we were able to follow the wall on its eastern side up to the northern wall of the enclosure and examine the layout of the gate complex, which included hypostyle halls and a transverse portico. It was thus possible to reconstruct the unexposed half of the gate and propose a comprehensive plan extending 70 meters in length and 46 meters in width (Fig. 52).

A wide corridor along the long axis, probably paved with mudbrick, was protected on either side by a series of ten bastions facing outward, directly accessible from the corridor. Several doors and a throne, preceded by a semicircular staircase, blocked the corridor and reduced it to little more than a meter in width, the throne itself taking up about 4 meters. The main entry at the northern end of the corridor was even narrower as it, too, was blocked by a throne supported by small buttresses.

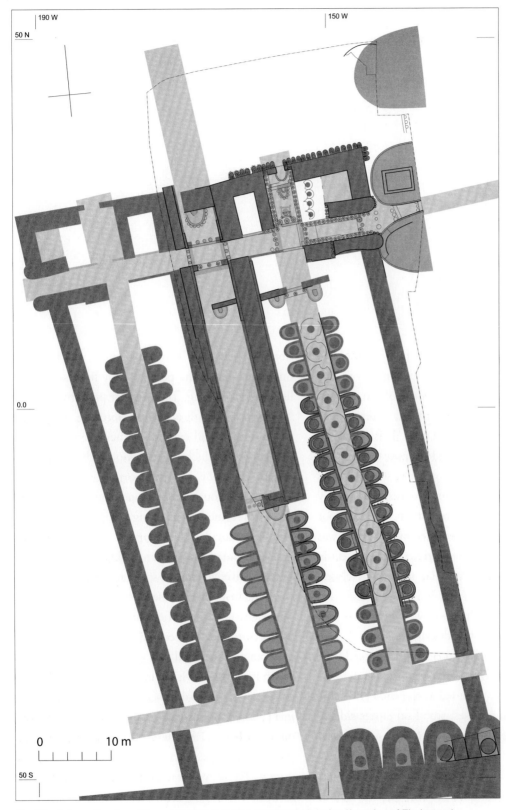

Fig. 52   Schematic plan of the northwest foregate constructed during the reign of Thutmose I

The secondary side corridor had a pavement of transverse brickwork; circular bases almost 4 meters in diameter took up the entire width of the passage. A central column about 1 meter in diameter was positioned in the center of each base. It is logical to assume that a long colonnade supported a lightweight roof over the corridor, from where troops were able to reach the bastions on either side. Shortly before the transverse northern portico, a central door barred passage. A throne preceded by a staircase was located on either side. The corridor then joined the portico, where a quadrangular space was closed off by four doors. The pivot holes and sockets for securing the leaves of the doors were preserved, but the southern doorway was damaged.

We have seen that the foregate was flanked by a portico that was well preserved on the east side. Two elongated bastions, rounded at the ends and reinforced by small buttresses, stood on either side of the entrance. The remains of pivot holes and a central socket indicate that the gate itself was slightly recessed. Along the entrance corridor itself we found circular earthen foundations, fashioned by hand, that supported a square central beam whose impres-

sion was still visible. This arrangement, which existed on both sides of the portico, may have supported lightweight roofing. The corridor probably led to a hypostyle hall with an axial colonnade. It is likely that a similar hall existed on the other side of the side corridor, which led to a door in the façade. Between this door and the portico, we uncovered hardened silt foundations supporting vertical beams; the latter formed a wall along the corridor and may also have provided roof support.

The foundations of a remarkable altar were visible in the relatively cramped space at the end of the side corridor. In its first phase, the pedestal of the altar was placed slightly to the south. It was then covered by a second altar, shifted slightly north. The original quadrangular pedestal was smaller than its replacement; its outline is visible in the circle formed by the column bases of a baldachin. The almost square original pedestal supported a circular feature, itself raised on a square base. An identical arrangement was uncovered in the sanctuary of the east temple of the *mnnw;* it is likely that these two examples supported a naos. In the case of the monumental entry, the location of the altar may have defined a cult area devoted to the protection of the city's defenders. The narrow spaces on either side of the baldachin must, however, have impeded traffic. Another noteworthy feature was aligned with the altar: a seat preceded by a staircase whose first rounded step was furnished with small buttresses; behind the seat, a semicircular step led to a doorway in the north façade.

The façade of the foregate was reinforced by an enormous wall that joined the transverse portico. This front was lined with a series of buttresses along its façade and turned sideways. The three openings of the foregate reveal the intent to distinguish this complex from the other military structures. Moreover, the presence of inner rooms in this pylon of sorts, so distinct from the bastioned construction of the foregate, indicates specific functions that remain to be defined. This was also the case for the large thrones, perhaps intended for important dignitaries responsible for access into the complex. This exceptional military structure does not seem to have been designed solely for defense; its organization has a ceremonial character as well, and the northern side up to the transverse corridor, while fortified, may have been used by the *mnnw* administration.

It is also worth noting that the central corridor, flanked by two low walls, was prolonged outside the building to the north. Geomagnetic survey revealed the underground traces of a large circular building at least 16 meters in diameter with an attached rectilinear feature (Fig. 48) extending directly toward the road from the foregate. We also observed, in the native eastern quarter of the *mnnw*, a building of similar plan with an entrance consisting of a long, somewhat narrow corridor. Geomagnetic survey has also suggested the presence of buttresses or bastions around this structure. The similar example in the city was certainly a cult installation; by analogy, we can assume that a religious structure existed at the approach to the foregate. In fact, in front of the northern foregate, we found traces of a similar building intended for a neighboring gate. The Egyptians thus preserved native places of worship both outside and inside the *mnnw*. Further excavation will allow us to confirm our hypothesis and identify the functions of these circular buildings.

These two projecting gates are surprising in their monumentality and the proportions they imparted to the defenses of the ceremonial city. Admittedly, we have only exposed the northern extent of the fortifications for less than 260 meters in length, but they must have enclosed an extensive area whose remains lie buried beneath agricultural fields. The Egyptian architects sought to enclose the African urban complex after destroying it, but the fortifications of the latter are as yet poorly understood: we have only a few points of reference from the geomagnetic survey. The African defensive system was more irregular. We found, around the outer northwest gate, earlier bastions some 40 meters long. Additional sondages will be necessary to better understand the military efforts undertaken by the Nubians or other African populations. The Egyptian intervention seems to correspond to a simplification, indeed almost an orthogonal schematization, of the previous fortifications. It was Egyptian models that guided the architectural program of the *mnnw.*

EGYPTIAN TEMPLES AND NATIVE CULT INSTALLATIONS

The sanctuary of the main temple of the religious complex erected after the conquest by Thutmose I corresponded to the center of the previous African city (Fig. 48). The location of three classically planned temples also took into consideration the location of the wells, which continued their religious functions. While the fortified native enclosures were intentionally destroyed, the northeast religious precinct was preserved. A large circular building may have followed the tradition of African places of worship, but further excavation is necessary to confirm this hypothesis and date the periods of occupation. Egyptian temples made up the central core of the *mnnw,* defining the major axis of the urban layout in line with the north gate. An extraordinary hypostyle hall connected the gate to the main temple in truly monumental fashion.

The three corridors of the gate continued through the hypostyle hall, which measured more than 50 by 20 meters inside and contained 144 columns in six rows on either side of a central corridor paved with mudbrick. The side walls were supported by connected bastions composed of low rounded walls. In its proportions the hall is comparable to the hypostyle hall at Karnak, built of stone and dating to the beginning of the Nineteenth Dynasty. As at Karnak, the hall at Dukki Gel functioned as a transitional space between the gate and the main temple. The great number of columns may be reminiscent of the "forest of columns" of earlier native palaces, and in particular Palace A. The column foundations of the Egyptian hall are equally deep but the bases of the shafts are larger in diameter, measuring 1.70 meters. Before the entrance to the central temple, in a passage along the axis, a central feature of brick was the starting point for a perpendicular road leading to a ceremonial palace.

The main temple was connected to the western temple by a peripteral colonnade that surrounded the two sanctuaries with their pronaos and hypostyle halls. The location of the temples took into account the two existing wells, whose waters continued to be accessible through an underground accommodation. The south well was incorporated into the double temple enclosure, with space to the south for a curved staircase and a corridor leading to one of the hypostyle halls. Two colonnaded porticos preceded the quadrangular religious precinct. These porticos were built against the thick wall of the façade, constricting the entrance to the hypostyle hall. The columns in the courtyards rested on wide bases, perhaps a function of the height of the shafts and the wall of the façade.

Joining the two sanctuaries by means of a peripteral colonnade was a typical architectural feature during the reign of Thutmose I. For a comparable plan we can turn to an almost contemporary example well known in Egypt: the Treasury of Thutmose I at Karnak, although constructed of sandstone and limestone while all the structures of Thutmose I at Dukki Gel were of mudbrick. Despite this significant difference, there are multiple comparisons between the plans: the original structure at Karnak, with its bark stand and a tripartite sanctuary, was surrounded by a peristyle and probably an external wall. This structure was added to the plan of the Treasury and became an integral part of it. Jean Jacquet proposed a date at the beginning of the Eighteenth Dynasty, in the reign of Ahmose or, more likely, Amenhotep I. This architectural feature may have been developed before Thutmose I and reached the height of its popularity during the reign of Hatshepsut.

Fig. 53   Detailed plan of the sanctuary of the east temple of Thutmose I

The two temples at Dukki Gel are apparent from their brick foundations, very well preserved on the floors, which were sometimes paved with brick. The west temple included a porticoed courtyard, a hypostyle hall with nine columns, a pronaos separated by a wall, and a sanctuary. An underground passage at the level of the water table of the south well ran along the west wall. At the end of this passage, a staircase led up to a basin in the hypostyle hall; to lessen the risk of collapse, the column of the pronaos over the underground passage was eliminated. The hypostyle hall of the main temple was larger, with thirty columns; a paved aisle emphasized the central axis of the plan. The location of a cross aisle is suggested by an enlarged space between the northern colonnades. The pronaos contained four columns located very close to an intermediate wall, so designed to leave sufficient space to access the sanctuary and its three colonnaded annexes. The sanctuary, which was slightly wider, may also have had a series of columns, but this layout cannot be confirmed due to the poor state of preservation.

The third annex of the sanctuary may have connected to the hypostyle hall. As in the neighboring temple, access was provided around the southern well to allow for the drawing of water; it was possible to follow the curvature of part of a staircase to a considerable depth. At the top of the stairs yet another staircase, located between the solid masses of an enormous wall, continued to the peripteral colonnade and the annex to reach the pronaos. The hydraulic systems of both temples indicate the importance of providing sacred water, probably to the hypostyle hall. There are several examples of temples with wells excavated inside the temenos, but they usually date to the Ptolemaic period; in our case the underground corridors are unique and were possibly associated with the cult of the god Amun, attested later in the two sanctuaries.

The east temple belongs to a later building phase; its side wall was built up against and incorporated, on the south side, the wall of the neighboring religious complex. The temple also included a separate peripteral colonnade enclosing a hypostyle hall, a fairly large pronaos, and a tripartite sanctuary (Fig. 53). The northern part of the temple, covered by the remains of Napatan and Meroitic religious structures, has not been excavated to any

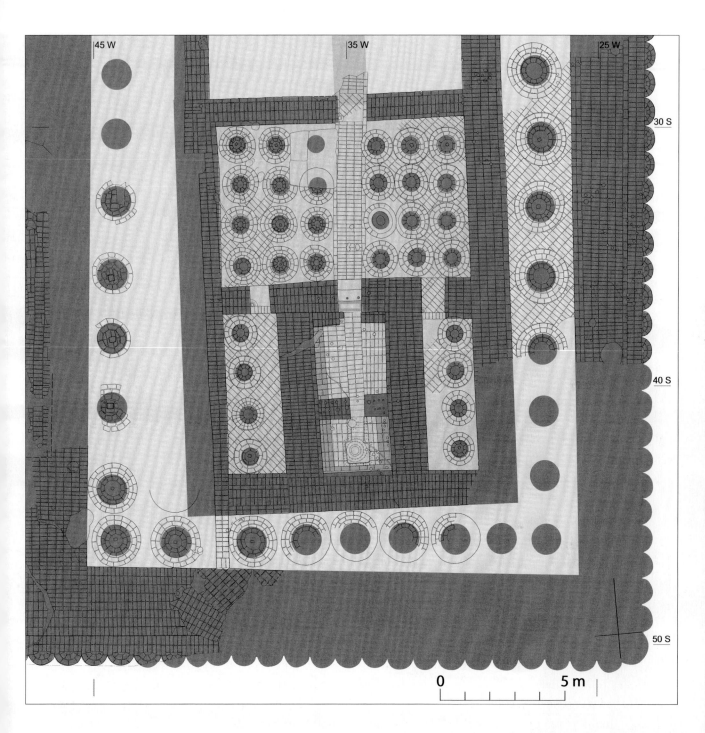

depth in order to preserve the later levels. Nevertheless, the stratigraphy of a Meroitic pit permitted a detailed analysis of occupational phases. Along the northern side of the peripteral colonnade, we found two column bases of the original temple, as well as the remnants of restoration work carried out under Hatshepsut and Thutmose III. Thick layers of sandstone fragments also allowed us to identify the destructions of the Amarna Period, which were followed by several restorations during the Nineteenth Dynasty and, finally, a Napatan surface.

Fig. 54   Detailed view of the east temple naos

The massive wall of the east temple was supported by external buttresses projecting for almost a meter. The thickness of the wall limited the space around the peripteral colonnade with its wide column bases. The hypostyle hall was not completely cleared to leave in place the bases of the mudbrick columns belonging to construction projects of Thutmose III. Sondages, however, revealed substantial supporting foundations belonging to Thutmose I, rebuilt in stone under Hatshepsut. Closer to the sanctuary, the pronaos of the neighboring buildings was replaced by a second hypostyle hall comprising six rows of four columns each. The column bases rested on a floor paved in angled bricks, as was also the case in the peripteral colonnade. In the central aisle, the pavement bricks were aligned in an orthogonal pattern.

It is unusual to be able to study the sanctuary of a temple; generally the holy of holies has been reconstructed several times and the original layout considerably modified. In our case, it appears that the sanctuary was preceded by a vestibule with benches placed on either side of the axial passage, which included several regular steps. The holiest room measured 2.70 by 2.10 meters; its space was further reduced by the presence of benches on three sides (Fig. 54). Four steps led through an intermediate door to a rectangular pedestal carefully coated with a layer of silt. Upon it was a circular pedestal of several handmade concentric rings of earth. These two pedestals were probably used as a base for a naos or altar. Oddly enough, dozens of small holes outlined these pedestals and steps, allowing us to reconstruct the placement of reeds used for marking or consolidation. The same plant stems were observed in the construction of thrones in the native palaces as well as the northwest foregate.

In front of the entrance wall of the sanctuary, another circular base may have supported a container. On the east side, a channel that led from the central pedestal served as a conduit for liquid, as indicated by the layers of sand found in the bottom of the evacuation system. We can therefore conclude that libations were poured around this altar and that liquid flowed through the channel to the peripteral portico. The benches may have been used for the placement of cult objects because their depth is not wide enough for sitting. A beer vessel recovered against one of the benches also supports their function as offering depositories. Although the temple was dismantled fairly early during the reign of Thutmose I, we did note a resumption of activity in the sanctuary when wooden stakes were installed along the length of the evacuation channel, probably after a collapse. Two colonnaded annexes completed the plan of the holy of holies.

The three temples founded during the construction of the *mnnw* formed a coherent architectural plan. The east temple was added almost immediately because the large hypostyle entry hall took it into account, as did the northeast palace (Fig. 55). The intent to give the east temple a special emphasis is fairly clear. Its outer wall was more elaborate, as was the peripteral colonnade. We note again that, with the succession of three hypostyle halls, greater regard was perhaps accorded to the god of this temple. The proximity of the native religious precinct probably caused some construction difficulties because the complexes are very close to each other. An enclosure wall was also built between these two complexes.

A chapel, located in front of the ramp of the north well, must also be mentioned in relation to the main religious precinct. The well arrangements and the towers of the enclosure were leveled to make room for a small building that sealed off the former passage and the fortifications of the native ceremonial center. The ramp itself remained in use as the entrance to the chapel was in the same location as the previous access. A thick wall on either side of the entry incorporated a small pylon of irregular dimensions opening onto a courtyard. The eroded surface yielded numerous ceramic deposits, mainly plates decorated with red slip and sometimes entirely covered with black slip. Several vessels were overturned on the ground. Since they were often deposited near corners, it is natural to consider them as offerings or foundation deposits. Scattered to the north but still part of the same deposit, fragments of incense burners, jar stands, and a few bread molds and miniature plates confirm the sacred character of the building.

Two rooms serving as a sanctuary opened onto the courtyard; a thick wall separated them and a single door probably existed to provide access to the southern room. A well-built wall delimited the southern side, and continued to the west. Against this wall, a series of storerooms must have extended as far as the western defenses, as yet poorly under-

stood in this area. Deposits containing ceramic material from the beginning of the Eighteenth Dynasty may have been associated with the construction of a fortified enclosure. Napatan workshops covered the southern area, and the segments of the New Kingdom enclosure recovered to date are insufficient for the interpretation of this complex without further excavation. These remains are of later date; only the chapel can be dated to the reign of Thutmose I.

Clearing in the northeast uncovered the complex remains of an area that underwent constant modification since its occupation by African and Nubian populations. Layers of mudbrick were superimposed in rapid succession, and we were able to determine that two oval religious buildings with two small chapels were contemporary with the first enclosure of the ceremonial city. The establishment of the *mnnw* did not lead to the destruction of this quarter; indeed, it is probable that the Egyptians, following a practice recognized elsewhere, allowed the local inhabitants to retain their places of worship. It was perhaps during the conquest and the destruction of

the palaces outside the city walls that a ceremonial palace was reconstructed next to the two cult installations. It was, in fact, only a matter of enlarging an existing building and adding a thick circular wall and a ring of columns. Two doors were oriented toward the entrances of neighboring cult buildings. It is likely that the original palace with its three seats, offering table, and baldachin was preserved inside the new circular wall.

The fortifications around this quarter are still in situ, and those on the west side were rebuilt along a rectilinear line. The entrance corridor of the cult building was also remodeled with new fortifications. This juxtaposition recalls the evidence of the geomorphological survey in the area of the northwest foregate. The liturgical facilities in these places of worship, with their thick buttresses supporting a vault, included pedestals beneath the naos and lightweight reinforcements that were more characteristic of features closely related to Egyptian installations. The native preference for a round plan is, however, quite distinct from the quadrangular architecture of the Pharaoh's master builders. We are left with the enigma of the large circular monument along the axis of the monumental northwest gate. A sondage along its perimeter indicates the presence of encircling connected bastions, an architectural feature comparable to other African cult installations. In addition, a road leading from the northwest gate to the circular building may indicate that the latter was in use at the beginning of the New Kingdom. The presence of a monumental entry would, once again, favor a cult belonging to the kingdoms to the south.

EGYPTIAN PALACES

We have seen that several of the ceremonial palaces constructed around the original city were leveled. The architect of the *mnnw* would, in turn, build two structures that functioned as palaces on either side of the associated religious complex. The first palace had access to roads leading to both the main and the east temples. By virtue of its location, the palace encroached upon parts of palaces A, B, and C (Fig. 56). The ceremonial roads were paved; one was oriented toward the large hypostyle hall and also

led to the central sanctuary. The other road, oriented toward the east temple, was preserved at its junction with the road to the palace. It is clear that the palace was directly related to two of the temples of the complex, thus confirming the ceremonial nature of the ensemble.

The entrance to the palace, with a double-leaved door, was through a massive wall that could almost be called a pylon. This entrance led to a hypostyle hall with sixteen columns and a cross wall with three doors. The central door, on the axis of the hall, was flanked by two projecting bastions; in the doorway were pivot holes identical to those found in numerous native buildings. These well-preserved pivot holes are evidence that local expertise influenced the Egyptian architects. A second hypostyle hall with eight columns continued to the next cross wall, also provided with three doors. The two side doors led to annexes with four columns each. The central door, also flanked by buttresses, led to a rounded platform with a step down into the throne room. This was a room of modest dimensions: the baldachin, reconstructed from its column bases, occupied all the available space. As a result, the two adjoining seats

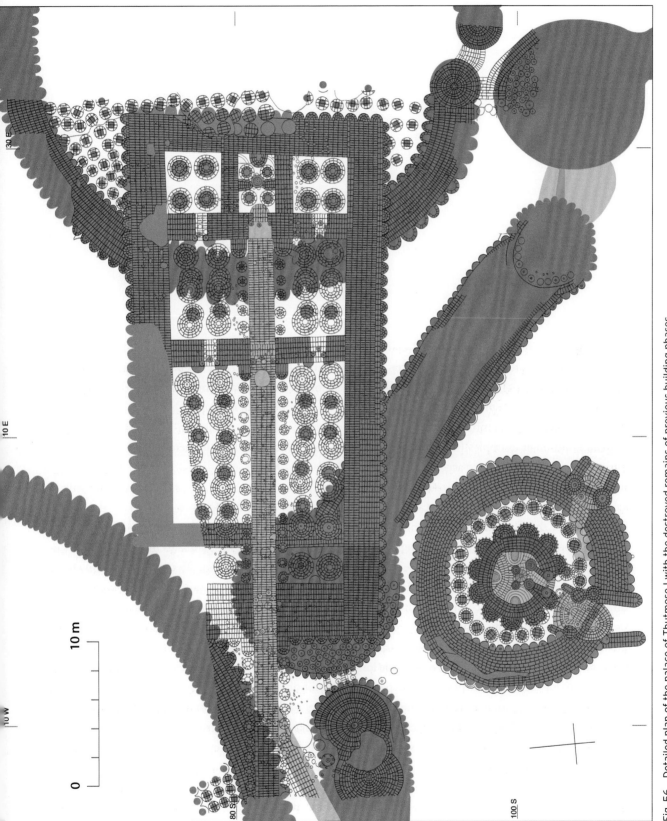

Fig. 56 Detailed plan of the palace of Thutmose I with the destroyed remains of previous building phases

and circular offering table were located below the canopy. As for the throne, preceded by a step, it appeared to be wedged against the eastern wall.

The ceremonial palace presents a very simple plan that must have been common during the New Kingdom, although examples from this period are quite rare in Egypt. Taking into account the building material, our palace would appear to be a simplified version of the structures that accompanied temples. The palaces of the Theban and Memphite regions certainly had more complex plans, depending on their functions and the will of the king. We recall the palace of Merenptah at Memphis, consisting of a long, rectangular building complex with a throne room rendered even more monumental by two colonnades and a raised platform covered by a canopy. The throne was approached by a ramp along the long axis and two side staircases. The plastered and painted decoration must have aroused the admiration of visitors. One part of the building was also reserved as a private apartment. This Nineteenth Dynasty example from Egypt was certainly richer, but as at Dukki Gel, it had a grand entry with colonnades occupying the length of the palace, followed by a throne room and,

finally, annexes useful to the life of a king. The scale is much reduced at Dukki Gel, where the palace was not occupied on a permanent basis. The modesty of the throne room is nevertheless remarkable and is, in fact, comparable to certain circular African buildings, which may have influenced, at least in part, the plan of Dukki Gel.

The second palace, to the south, is more difficult to interpret. It is connected to the back of the central temple by a long staircase along the axis but slightly diverted off course to line up with the entrance to the building. That entrance follows the African tradition, with two towers framing the door. The diameters of the towers differ, as also observed at the entrances to the ceremonial city. The entrance courtyard, trapezoidal in plan, had four colonnades with five column bases each. The central aisle was built on a slope, and a central staircase led from one level to the next. A second door, once again flanked by massive rounded structures, opened onto a hypostyle hall with fifty-seven columns (Fig. 57). On the west side the plan was more irregular, with a trapezoidal hypostyle hall with twenty columns. On the long axis, small columns in the corridor decreased its

width. This corridor continued between two annexes with four columns each. The throne room was disturbed by Napatan walls, but we also found, in this location, the older remains of a small native palace.

This palace was destroyed during the reconquest by the Nubian coalition. Reddened by a violent conflagration, the masonry was profoundly disturbed. We have noted that the exterior wall and the two entry towers were lined with connected buttresses, like the external walls of the northeast palace. The architectural irregularities of the south building lead us to believe that local labor was employed, perhaps under the direction of a Nubian foreman. The overall construction of the *mnnw* required a significant effort, and the choice of architectural solutions was affected by simultaneous building activities over a vast extent. It is necessary to locate the fortified south side in order to understand how work proceeded in this sector. It appears, upon first consideration, that conflict was very violent in this location, which may explain why a more advanced defensive system was constructed on top of the ruins of the south palace.

An enclosure walled off a group of twenty silos, which represented a considerable food reserve. It was situated on the location of Palace A, and it was still possible to observe portions of the palace walls and corridors. The silo walls, 3 to 4 meters in diameter, were consolidated by ten or so widely spaced small buttresses; we can estimate their height at 5 meters at least. Often depicted on bas-reliefs, these granaries are known in Egypt and have been found in numerous archaeological sites. The remains suggest that they pertain to an Egyptian model, but the buttresses may have been a local addition. This storage complex, part of the *mnnw*, was destined to feed the troops, but also provided on-the-spot reserves of local grain. According to the excavations at Gism el-Arba by Brigitte Gratien, the silos of that region were of an entirely different type, with wooden structures and external staircases.

Fig. 58   The northeast palace of Thutmose I during restoration

Floor-level water channels paved with angled brick occupied the space between the storage complex and the large hypostyle entry hall. A basin was connected to these features. Built against the enclosure wall, it probably collected rain runoff from the top of the fortifications. Another shallow circular basin, 5 meters wide, provided an excellent watering place. This area contained numerous drinking troughs for animals. The Aswan stela from the reign of Thutmose II mentions the flocks that Thutmose I kept in his *mnnw*. Careful scrutiny of the area revealed hundreds of bovine hoofprints. These hydraulic installations trampled by animals provide convincing proof that some portion of the flocks was housed next to the storage area.

On the other side of the entry axis, an enormous pottery workshop probably also belonged to the Egyptian administration. Here we found several kilns as well as installations for the processing of clay. A thick layer of sherds covers the reworked remains of Palace G. Judging by its size, this workshop certainly had a considerable output. Wheel-made pottery of buff-colored fabric and numerous painted pieces correspond to New Kingdom styles that complete the assemblage of this period, during which the ceramic production of the Kerma cultures was destined to disappear. Although lacking a significant portion of the fortifications, we must keep in mind the distinctive quality of the *mnnw*. It was an institution that absorbed the ceremonial city, with new and impressive Egyptian buildings preserving native functions. The main cult installations of the African and Nubian populations, tolerated by the invaders, remain to be discovered (Fig. 58).

THE BLACK KINGDOM OF THE NILE

The Resumption of Power by the King of Kerma and His Allies

From the Aswan stela we learn what happened in ancient Pnubs under Thutmose II: three war chieftains pillaged the *mnnw* of Thutmose I. Archaeological excavation has shed some light on this transitional period, which saw the return of African-style structures and the systematic destruction of monuments belonging to the Egyptian administration. Considerable effort was expended on the defense of several buildings, but our limited intervention prevented us from fully understanding the consequences of this resumption of power, which did not, in any case, last for long. We have primarily documented the fortification systems, and our presentation can only be provisional (Fig. 59).

See following page for Fig. 59

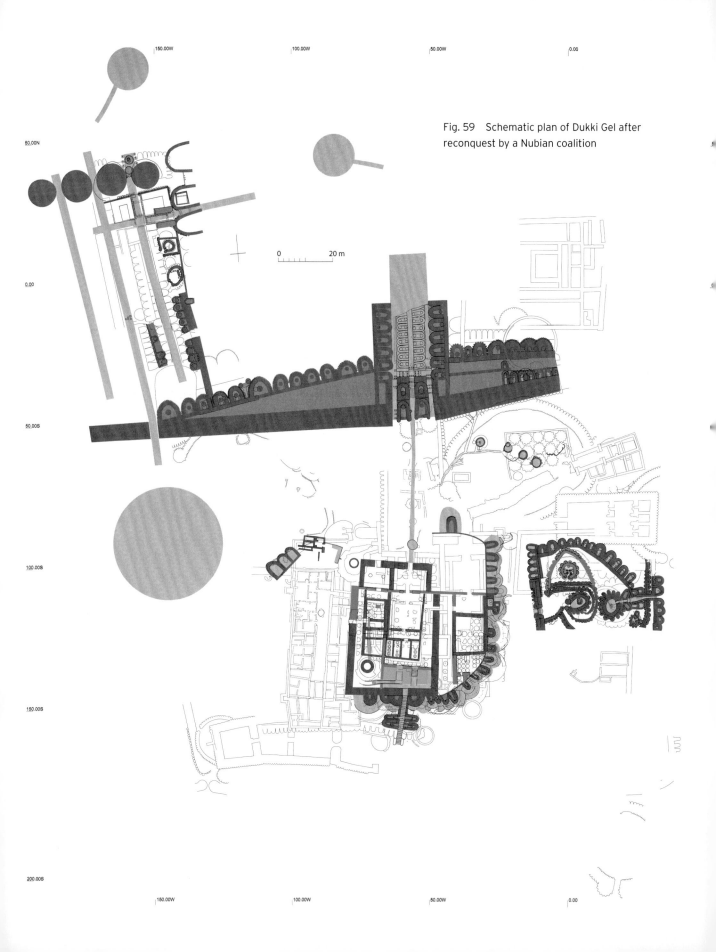

150.00W 100.00W 50.00W 0.00

50.00N

0.00

50.00S

100.00S

150.00S

200.00S

Fig. 59   Schematic plan of Dukki Gel after reconquest by a Nubian coalition

0   20 m

Nubian and African Remains after Thutmose I

FORTIFICATIONS

On either side of the north gate, a new fortification line faced outward. Its thick wall, lined with a series of large connected bastions, truncated the ends of the bastions belonging to the former fortifications of Thutmose I. The bastions of the new defensive system were as deep as they were wide, almost semicircular in shape. The rounded walls were supported by small round buttresses. The line of bastions turned inward at the north foregate to protect the central passage. The alterations to the northwest foregate were different in nature because, along the fortified east wall, the series of bastions turning into the central passage was interrupted to make space for some unusual constructions connected by a narrow wall.

One of these constructions, protected by a quadrangular enclosure, has a circular interior plan. The enclosure opened to the southwest through a door with uprights on oval bases. Small buttresses lined the wall; semicircular in shape, they were supported by a square vertical beam. Numerous postholes were found around the rounded foundations of the doorway. Wider beams supported the heavy up-

rights. A rounded mass measuring 1.50 meters made up the threshold; crossing it, one reached a second door in a circular wall more than 1 meter thick. The doorway narrowed, with a flat threshold measuring 0.60 meters and flanked by two small rounded uprights supported by a vertical beam. Construction was careful, with several wood elements still visible.

Next one entered into an interior space (Fig. 60). This circular structure, about 5 meters in diameter with an empty interior more than 2.50 meters in diameter, provided shelter to soldiers. Troops could access an upper platform by means of a staircase with at least five steps, whose rectangular base is still traced by several series of aligned bricks. This base was reinforced with closely spaced wooden boards, which also served to consolidate the upper level. Stakes along the rounded outer wall added to the strength of the wall, which was probably surmounted by merlons. The size of this structure is surprising: it was probably no more than 3 or 4 meters high and constituted a relatively weak point of defense. It is, however, not impossible that wooden superstructures completed it. Four more similar constructions

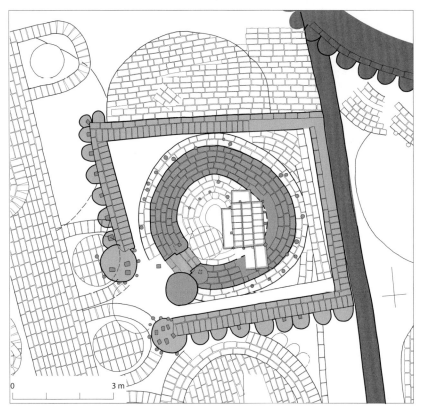

Fig. 60   Detailed plan of native fortifications

were partially exposed along the alignment of the Egyptian foregate.

We are left with the impression that an overall plan was imposed at the beginning of the reign of Thutmose I and that after the conflicts with the native coalition the foregate was rebuilt using the same defensive system, with no attempt being made to unify the fortifications. We also lack a detailed plan of the remains identified by the geomagnetic survey immediately to the east, where the bastions belonged to a very different system. Equally noteworthy is the fact that below the fortification works just described, the remains of two oval bastions belonged to a system of defensive walls supported by connected buttresses. The bastions turn against themselves and do not follow the usual plan of defensive works at Dukki Gel. The last fortified recess studied in this area was almost on the same alignment. It resembles

the one in the north and is superimposed over a former structure. Oval in plan, its wall was reinforced by massive rounded buttresses that supported a beam surrounded by a silt facing. The entrance had two thick uprights on either side of a threshold with pivot holes. A wider staircase occupied the interior shaft; all around it masses of hardened earth supported vertical beams. There, too, wooden constructions must have existed, but we have yet to understand them. The architectural tradition to which they belong remains to be studied.

Following the structures to the north, we found the remains of several large circular foundations, just perceptible beneath a wide reworked façade. Between these massive constructions, a rectilinear threshold and the closing device for a door with double leaves were still in place. Continuing to follow the line of the side passage, we were able to

Fig. 61   Aerial view of the entrance of the foregate of the coalition with the offering circle

reconstruct two entry towers in front of the foregate abandoned under Thutmose I. Cult installations, partially revealed, were located in the entry space. Two large circles meant for offerings were placed almost in the gateway, one right against the threshold, the other 1 meter farther to the exterior. The latter was under a canopy whose light roofing was supported by six columns. Still farther away, other circles appeared after scraping. All these circular features were lined with small connected buttresses, similar to the offering tables we have already seen. We observed in the center of some of these features quadrangular pedestals enclosed within a small circle with edges scalloped with compacted earth (Fig. 61).

Although this façade had African-style towers, it belonged to the architectural transformation imposed by the Egyptian conquerors. Reconstructing the totality of modifications carried out by the regional power is complicated, but we do know that the foremen used a portion of the existing fortifications while making certain adjustments. The offering deposits in front of the new façade evoke a

ceremonial rite connected to cult practices, while military functions were served by multiple fortifications. This duality was already evident under Thutmose I, when an altar was located a few meters beyond the line of a side corridor. Are we to believe that cult practices took place in the foregates, adding another function to their ceremonial and military roles? Several large circular foundations indicate the locations of monumental gates or fortified walls that incorporated aligned towers from earlier periods.

The remains of three older bastions, 40 meters in length, were found along the northwest foregate. They were built up against the defensive system of the original city. Although we lack a complete understanding of this fortification turned toward the foregate, we can assume that portions of the older works remained in use or were reused by the native coalition, as the roads were maintained in this direction. It is quite clear that the two grand entrances on the north side of the city were still favored by Nubians and Africans. The coalition of the three war chieftains considered these gates to be an integral

Fig. 62 Fortified front of the coalition

part of the fortifications: their military, and probably religious, function had to be maintained since they were apparently associated with the most important cult buildings.

In the ceremonial city, the east temple was sacrificed to make way for a fortified line of closely spaced bastions, and an entry was added to create a cross passage (Fig. 62). The line of bastions turned to the north and south. Apparently the allies wanted to protect the sacred place where the Egyptians had erected their temples, the site that constituted the central core of their city. Rebuilding during the New Kingdom in this spot has prevented us from finding the remains of cult buildings belonging to the transitional phase. The brevity of this period may have precluded the construction of a major building in this religious precinct, and the central and west temples may have been preserved. Fortifications were, however, expanded on the south side and defenses added to the axial staircase, while the neighboring Egyptian palace was destroyed.

The native religious precinct in the northeast, incorporated into the architectural program of the

mnnw of Thutmose I, underwent an extraordinary transformation. The two places of worship and the palace were protected in a surprising manner. Along the layout of the leveled native city, connected bastions formed a powerful external line of defense. This fortified front, which turned toward the inner enclosure equipped with a gate, was oriented toward the center of the complex where the Egyptian temples were located and the fortifications faced the opposite direction. Several bastioned enclosures completed the defenses; their layout was adjusted to accommodate the existing oval and circular buildings. The palace itself was scaled down in size and restored to the plan of the original structure, which had been preserved inside of the round columned building. The entry corridor of the main sanctuary was fortified with several bastions.

CULT BUILDINGS

In the northeast religious precinct, the buildings were surrounded by fortifications that underwent several modifications. Enclosures were doubled

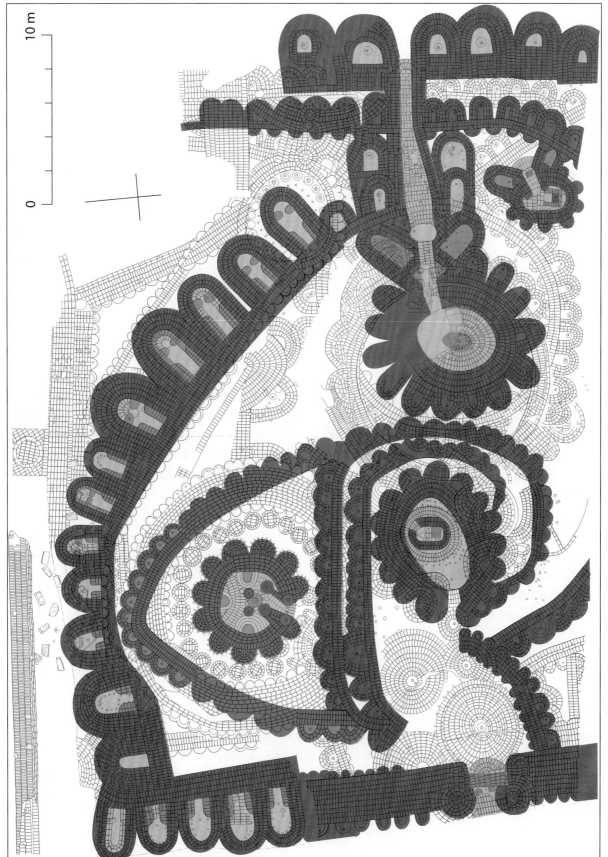

Fig. 63   Detailed plan of the modifications undertaken to the fortifications in the northeast religious precinct

around buildings despite the external defensive system (Fig. 63). To the east, no fewer than four successive lines of defense barred passage. The effort expended on fortification proves that the inhabitants feared the worst and their places of worship were under threat. Geomagnetic survey revealed two circular buildings to the north, each with an entry corridor into a central space lined with buttresses along the perimeter. The corridors faced the roads leading to the north and northwest gates. While our assumption remains to be confirmed, we can acknowledge that cult installations were located along the roads leading into the city and were provided with protected entry corridors.

We should also consider, in this context, the large circular monument located outside the original enclosure of the native city but probably associated with the distinctive northwest gate. We were able to confirm that this circular structure was buttressed along its perimeter. The Egyptians certainly expended a great deal of effort on the foregate that faced the circular structure, which leads us to suppose that the latter was exceptional in character. It fell into

disuse in the second half of the Eighteenth Dynasty and was thereafter used as a *zeriba* or animal pen; cattle hoofprints were evident in the damp mud. We should, however, consider this oval or circular building to be one of the original focal points of urbanization at Dukki Gel. We believe that it was a cult installation that was certainly reconsecrated during the period of transition.

Archaeological investigation has provided clear evidence that the three war chiefs of the coalition destroyed the establishments of Thutmose I. Horizontal stratigraphy has revealed the extent of urban development and the succession of fortifications, and layers of destruction and reconstruction supplement this relative chronology. Our hypotheses suggest a period of very short duration, so it is not surprising that the depth of deposit is very shallow. Large mudbrick structures may have been completely eroded by the wind, and the reuse of brick has precluded a comprehensive interpretation of the typically shallow foundations. While this transitional period remains difficult to understand, several important monuments are sure to yield additional information.

PART III

Pnubs during the New Kingdom, Napatan, and Meroitic Periods

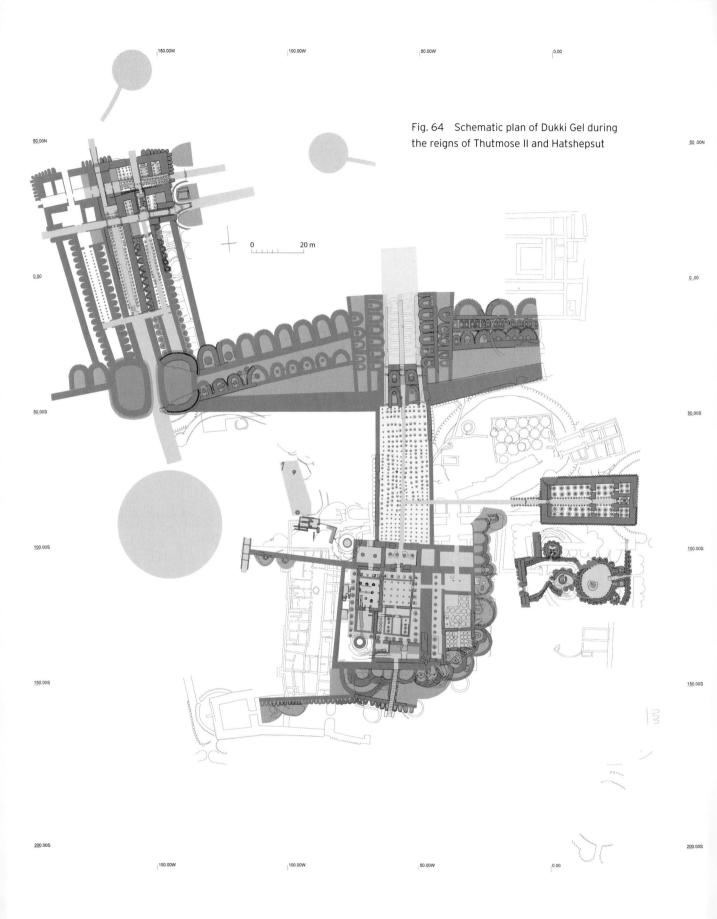

Fig. 64   Schematic plan of Dukki Gel during the reigns of Thutmose II and Hatshepsut

50.00N

0.00

50.00S

100.00S

150.00S

200.00S

150.00W   100.00W   50.00W   0.00

50.00N

0.00

50.00S

100.00S

150.00S

200.00S

0   20 m

Restoration of the *mnnw* by Thutmose II and Hatshepsut

To pay respect to and honor their father, first Thutmose II and then Hatshepsut rebuilt the *mnnw*. Although the buildings expanded in scale, the architect preserved the general plan of the original complex. The south palace was torn down to make way for an enlarged fortification system. Although the ensemble was transformed and buildings leveled, the new *mnnw* stood on almost exactly the same spot as its predecessor. It is difficult to understand how the architect was able to maintain the walls on their original alignment, or how buildings were restored while preserving parts of the former structures. Perhaps some walls remained after the seizure of power by the native coalitions, but closer examination of the foundations leaves us with the distinct impression that all the walls had been removed before the start of the second Egyptian building program. It is possible that not all the earlier brickwork had been salvaged before the new Egyptian program began and that, in fact, the buildings of Thutmose I had been only partially dismantled (Fig. 64).

Construction must have been carried out by builders under the supervision of an architect who was probably involved in the building of the first *mnnw*. The institution was so powerful that the original building program was continued, with the addition of modifications considered necessary after the recent conflicts. According to the accepted chronology, Thutmose I ruled approximately twelve or thirteen years. The reign of his son Thutmose II lasted only four years, and the reign of Hatshepsut, daughter of Thutmose I, began right after it. If the Aswan stela is to be believed, the *mnnw* was destroyed during the reign of Thutmose I, so we can date the beginning of its reconstruction to Thutmose II, followed by Hatshepsut. The reconquest of Pnubs by the Nubio-African coalition could only have occurred during a ten-year span, a very short period of time that primarily saw the construction of fortification works at the site.

It is rare indeed, from an archaeological point of view, to find a building ensemble leveled and then rebuilt on an almost identical plan. In addition, a historical text mentions this episode of transfer of power. We must also add that the architectural styles of the Nubian, African, and Egyptian populations were different enough to leave behind marked singularities. When all the buildings are oval or circular, followed by Egyptian or Nubian structures on a square or rectangular plan that persisted into the modern period, it is not that difficult to reconstruct the main currents of influence. But once the methods of construction came from Central Africa, where the periods in question remain unknown, our basis for comparison is extremely limited (Fig. 56).

The building project begun by Thutmose II was impressive; its remains are substantial enough to provide an image of a *mnnw* along grander proportions. Given the brevity of the reign of Thutmose II, we can assume that it was Hatshepsut who completed the construction, as confirmed by epigraphic studies. The use of stone increased little by little, principally under Hatshepsut. Indeed, the project continued to evolve, and certain features, such as the northwest gate, were impressive additions. In comparing the two building programs, it is clear that an additional effort was associated with the reconstruction. On the one hand, there was an elevated military response with even more imposing fortifications and, on the other, a multiplication of columns in the great hypostyle hall.

NORTHERN FORTIFICATIONS

The fortified enclosure of the city was reconstructed with an additional line of defense. After the wall with connected bastions of Thutmose I, followed by the wall built by the African and Nubian coalition, a new bastioned wall was established along the perimeter. Three enclosure walls thus faced the surrounding countryside. The fortifications were adapted to gate structures where necessary and wall orientation varied according to need. This last fortified front was reinforced with powerful bastions projecting 9 meters outward and supporting a wall only 2 meters thick. Once again, circular supports were set up inside the structures to facilitate construction. The fortifications were built right up against the north gate, whose defenses were doubled on either side. A complementary front flanked by wider bastions was also added to the east during this period. These two building stages appear to belong to the reigns of Thutmose II and Hatshepsut, respectively, as they reflect different architectural choices.

NORTHWEST GATE AND FOREGATE

The three enclosures are interrupted on the west side by a gigantic gate that covered earlier building stages. The proportions of this gate, which measures 23 by 35 meters, are indeed exceptional. Two oval towers were arranged on either side of a relatively narrow passage only 2 meters wide. Visible in the interior masonry is a wall face more than 2 meters thick and a brick-paved floor. Staircases probably led to platforms for troops and to passages linking the walls of the city. Before entering the complex, one had to pass through the foregate established by Thutmose I (Fig. 65). This construction increased in monumentality with the addition of a massive façade more than 12 meters in length, resulting in a total length of 100 meters for the gate and its foregate. The width of the three parallel passages of the foregate did not change, but a double colonnade replaced the single colonnade of the side passage. Likewise, the central passage was widened and lined with colonnades on either side. While the ceremonial aspect is most evident in the central part of the foregate, the rows of connected bastions are evidence of a military

intent to keep an eye on traffic along the passages. Longitudinal walls were also part of this defensive system, but the cross partitions and thrones disappeared almost entirely from the central sector, where there must have been a passage linking the three corridors.

The former body of the Thutmose I façade was incorporated into a second structure belonging to the façade of the foregate built during the reign of Hatshepsut (Fig. 66). These two architectural complexes were separated by two transverse corridors. The earlier of the two completely isolated the façade; numerous doors blocked this corridor, which ended in a double bastion protecting the side entrance. The second corridor, also ending in a double-bastioned side entrance, was flanked by two rows of columns. The first phase of this corridor had only a single colonnade. Each of these corridors led to hypostyle halls; the ones in the northeast corner comprised two rows of four column bases. Thrones preceded by several steps were found along the axis. Here, too, several series of axial columns indicate a previous roofing phase. Toward the center of the complex, a hypostyle hall of sixteen columns

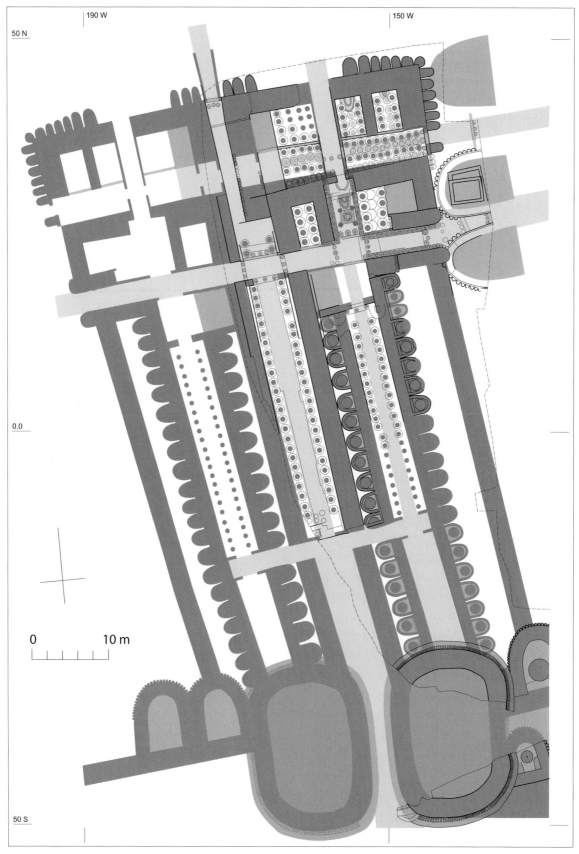

Fig. 65   Schematic plan of the northwest foregate constructed by Thutmose II and Hatshepsut

Fig. 66 Aerial view of the façade complex of the northwest foregate

belonged to a more important feature, perhaps associated with a staircase to the upper terrace around the wall of the façade and intended for the defense of the foregate. Other stairs remain to be identified in these two building complexes. Long, narrow buttresses supported the length of the façade and followed its contours. We can surmise that these buttresses were inclined inward and did not exceed the height of the terrace. Arrangements for fastening the closing device of the central gate, with its two leaves, have been preserved as well as the threshold. These arrange-

ments were extended to the north by a narrow-walled passage. The entrance on the east side no longer exists, but a wide corridor indicates its position. Beyond the first façade, after a second gate with a rounded step, the passage continued up to a canopied altar. This altar, with its circular base, was located on an older consecrated spot. Since this liturgical installation occupied all the available space, we must ask ourselves if it was, in fact, even possible to walk around this chapel of sorts to enter the adjacent hypostyle hall. The remnants of a throne

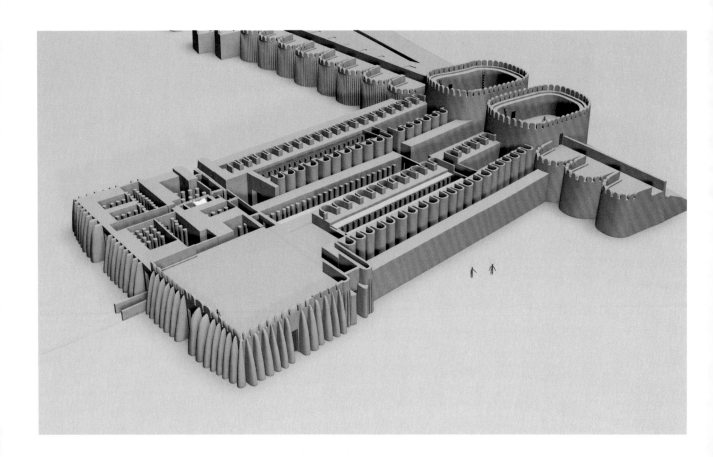

foundation were located north of the altar. Almost on the same spot but in the axial corridor, a monumental throne with semicircular steps was also erected during this new building phase.

As we only had access to the eastern half of the gate and foregate, we have reconstructed the plan of the entire complex with the inclusion of a secondary passage to the west. It is worth noting that the foregate was almost 50 meters wide, with another 55 meters added to the body of the façade. This astounding New Kingdom structure appears to be an Egyptianizing adaptation of the entry vestibules known from building complexes of the second half of the Classic Kerma Period. We have, however, proposed that the grand constructions of Dukki Gel were the work of peoples from central Sudanese kingdoms. It is almost certain that the occupation by the coalitions of the Third Cataract began much sooner, during the Middle Kingdom.

The Egyptian foregate and gate are comparable to examples from Buhen and Mirgissa (Emery 1973, pl. 3; Gratien 1990, V:fig. 73). This was an architecture designed to impress the native population. We have noted the military role of successive defensive fronts (Monnier 2010, fig. 93). Equally noteworthy were the ceremonial aspects of these buildings, with their passages flanked by columns; a religious function is probably suggested by the hypostyle halls, thrones, and altars. It is worth recalling that during the period of transition, one of the gates was preceded by offering tables and, most likely, altar pedestals (Fig. 67).

SOUTHERN FORTIFICATIONS

Around the three Egyptian temples, the fortifications of the transitional period were reworked. A much stronger front replaced the previous defensive

Fig. 67   Reconstruction of the northwest gate after the
building projects of Thutmose II and Hatshepsut

line of small bastions. The new bastions, 10 meters wide, formed a connected line that was a bit irregular but nevertheless solid. The eastern front continued to the north, where several transformations were carried out. This area exhibited traces of fire, and toppled masonry was left abandoned, perhaps the result of a war during the New Kingdom. Other remains were partially uncovered to the west, where a thick fortified wall and the foundations of a passage remain to be interpreted. An expanded southern front included a long enclosure, widening to the northwest, with many connected bastions.

EGYPTIAN TEMPLES AND NATIVE PLACES OF WORSHIP

The large hypostyle hall of the entrance was completely leveled, then reconstructed on exactly the same spot. The number of columns was, however, doubled, with ten rows of thirty supports, numbering 300 in all. A few columns were preserved up to 0.80 meters in height, and we were able to determine that the mudbrick shafts measured 0.60 to 0.70 meters in diameter on bases 1 meter wide. The central passage

was paved with brick. Construction techniques were similar to those of the previous palaces, with deep foundations ensuring the stability of the columns. The local architectural tradition must certainly have influenced this multiplicity of columns. The side walls of the hypostyle hall were rebuilt along the exact line of the previous foundations. The traffic pattern barely changed, with entry into the complex through the corridors of the north gate, a perpendicular passage leading to the palace, and access to the main temple in the center (Fig. 68).

The temenos of the double temple was enlarged to the west, but the peripteral portico remained on the same location. The quadrangular outline was maintained, although the previous columns were removed. The layout of the two temples resembled that of the first plan, but the two hypostyle halls were provided with sandstone pillars on circular bases also of sandstone. Surprisingly, the columns of the peripteral portico adjoining the hypostyle halls were also furnished with stone pillars on the north and east sides. The older columns of the colonnade of Thutmose I, except for the ones that were replaced, were preserved in situ although their bases

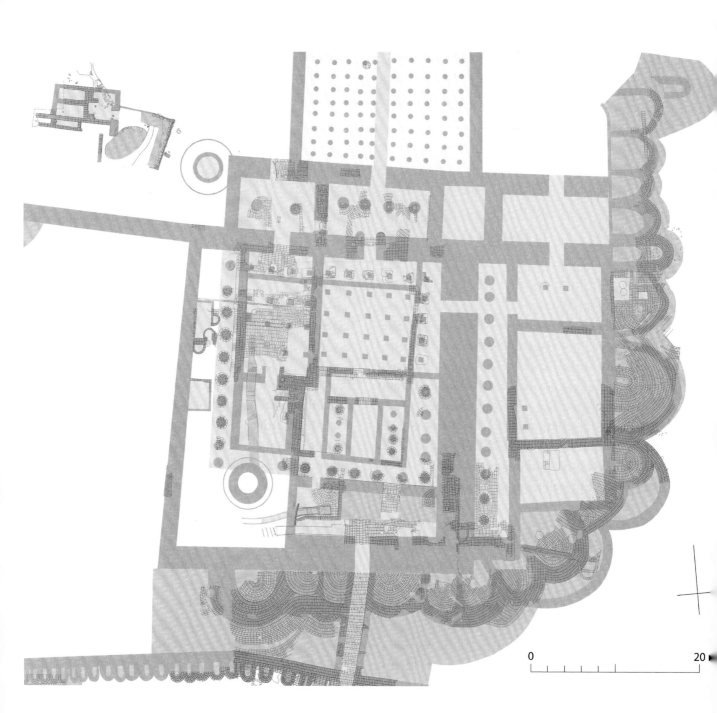

0   20

Fig. 68 Detailed plan of the temples under Thutmose II
and Hatshepsut

were enlarged, evidence that the columns had been dismantled. These modifications are evident in the west and south parts of the complex, and partially in the east part. The peripteral portico thus lost its previous unity in order to increase the grandeur of the hypostyle halls. The new stone supports of the portico alternated with the razed columns; in contrast, the stone bases in the halls themselves were laid out according to a different plan (Badawy 1968, 282–292).

These pillars, probably decorated during the reign of Hatshepsut, do not always have circular bases in situ, as in the west temple. The bases were placed on a foundation of coarse, irregular blocks in a wide trench. Traces of the lower parts of the pillars are still visible on the bases. The trenches dug along the peripteral portico were either rectangular with rounded corners or circular; in the central temple, the trenches were filled with large fragments of foundation blocks systematically broken up during the later reconstructions by Thutmose III. In the central axis, however, at the location of the north gate erected during construction in the portico, two bases were kept in place. One was located under

a door jamb, the other in the center of the threshold. The two courtyards at the entrance to the temples were similar in plan to their predecessors, with the columns of the portico preserving the original layout.

In the west temple, fragments of a brick floor were preserved in the entrance courtyard. So were parts of the peripteral portico and the hypostyle hall, separated by a partition. While the first row of two engaged pillars and two circular bases and central pillars are in situ, the next two rows could only be reconstructed from the layout of their brick foundations. Southwest of the hypostyle hall, two bases were missing to make room for the opening of the staircase from the underground passage to the south well. A monolithic stone altar and terra-cotta basin were also found in this location. In the southeast corner of the hall, a whitewashed surface had been renewed several times. In the opposite corner, in the northwest, traces of this white coating were also preserved, here associated with a channel probably leading from the north well. This small channel, passing through the portico to the west, must then have turned toward the neighboring well. The hypostyle hall was thus supplied with water from the two large wells. The channel passed in front of a thick, large sandstone slab that may have been used as the pedestal for a side altar.

The hypostyle hall led to the sanctuary, which appears to have consisted of a single room with a completely whitewashed floor. The wide doorway was probably accented by low walls, part of a porch of sorts in the hypostyle hall. Inside the sanctuary doorway, a space was provided for the deposit of offerings. Several cult objects were arranged along the east wall, notably a private stela dedicated to "Amun-Ra, lord of Pnubs," representations of ears, a ram protome painted yellow, a small bronze ram's head from a "sacred staff," and six uninscribed stelae (Valbelle 2005b, 251–254). Several deposits of vessels were arranged along the wall, including flat-based plates placed vertically against the wall and ceramic goblets overturned on the ground.

The entrance courtyard to the central temple had a wide transverse portico built under Thutmose I. Two of its enormous columns were preserved to a height of 0.50 and 0.80 meters. They were probably reused after destruction by the native coalition. The courtyard was paved with bricks arranged askew. The door leading to the peripteral portico was remodeled on a monumental scale, with two bastions with massive semicircular projections. In the portico itself the brick columns were replaced by pillars on circular bases, one of which was located directly in line with the doorway. Passing a partition, one entered the hypostyle hall, where we were able to reconstruct the location of the column bases from the position of the two rows of sandstone pillars of the peripteral portico. Several mounds of alluvial soil helped us locate the colonnades of Thutmose I, but Hatshepsut's hypostyle hall was completely destroyed by construction under Thutmose III, with the reexcavation of the foundation trenches.

On the south side of the hypostyle hall, a doorway, the sandstone slab of its threshold still in place, led to a pronaos. We do not know if the previous columns of the pronaos were reconstructed, but in any case no columns remain. The tripartite sanctuary was easily accessible, as well as the two annexes on either side of the holy of holies, where their axial colonnades are preserved. On the other hand, the sanctuary space itself was apparently completely empty. A fourth oblong room located on the west side of the west sanctuary had a carefully white-washed floor. This room led to a staircase, excavated next to the south well, that provided access through the portico to the hypostyle hall. We followed the remains of the staircase as it circled around the well down to the water table, enclosed within stone masonry. The stairwell led into a secluded room that maintained the previous layout in its entirety after the abandonment of a first staircase.

Thus we have proof that the two temples were equipped with protected passages that ensured the supply of sacred water to the hypostyle halls. The access corridors, serving the functions of the cult of Amun, were independent of the sanctuary and its annexes. Behind the sanctuary itself, an extremely thick wall continued along the length of the peripteral portico. Traffic was reestablished into the portico, in particular through a wide doorway several steps high. This doorway provided access to the southern fortifications, in the middle of which an extremely long staircase led to the site of the second palace, now completely destroyed. This remarkable axial staircase passed through the two defensive lines aligned with the fortifications of the northern fore-gate, large hypostyle hall, and central temple, but we do not know how or where these fortifications culminated in the south.

The sanctuary of the east temple was torn down to make way for a bastioned front around the Egyptian religious complex of the *mnnw*. What remains of these fortifications, constructed after the coalition conquest, is conserved to no more than 20 centimeters in height above layers contemporary with Thutmose I. After systematic mapping, we were able to remove these structures to reveal the remains of the earlier temple. Once we observed that the bastions had been rebuilt and enlarged, we were in a position to propose a new plan for the reconstructions under Thutmose II and Hatshepsut. The peripteral portico was abandoned to the east and south, replaced by immense semicircular bastions that left behind a mass of mudbrick covering a considerable surface. Oddly enough, contrary to the practice of maintaining sacred spaces, the sanctuary of Thutmose I was also abandoned. In this case the fortifications were obviously the priority, and in the hypostyle hall preceding the former sanctuary, a new holy of holies, possibly tripartite, was installed.

In front of the latter, a very large hypostyle hall was preserved. The foundations for the columns were laid under Thutmose III. Destruction trenches 0.80 meters deep have revealed traces of mudbrick foundations dating to Thutmose I. These remains were covered by thick layers of sandstone fragments, probably belonging to pillars from Hatshepsut's reign. In this location as well, there was a large hypostyle hall that remains to be excavated and planned. A large sondage to the north confirmed the existence of a passage along the peripteral portico, where stratigraphy has revealed the presence of two reworked pillars. The passage led to a side door opening into the middle of an older fortification system refurbished with a tower. The entrance courtyard of the east temple, located beneath the remains of Napatan and Meroitic temples, remains to be found.

The fences and bastioned enclosures of the northeast religious precinct were partially dismantled. The fortifications, although less effective, were maintained along the periphery. The principal place of worship was rebuilt with a larger diameter of 16 meters; inside the enclosure a portion of the former building was preserved. Well-developed bastions encircled the slightly irregular oval hall, and the entry passage was protected by four side bastions up to the bastioned enclosure that constituted the eastern front. The center of the second native place of worship was reworked with a low circular wall protecting the pedestal of the naos. A double row of posts was subsequently installed to consolidate this arrangement. The palace belonging to this complex may be preserved next to the places of worship.

THE PALACE OF HATSHEPSUT

Like the great hypostyle hall at the entrance to the central Egyptian temple and its avenue leading toward the palace, this entire sector of the *mnnw* precinct was leveled. The palace, although rebuilt along the same proportions, was nevertheless extended to the west (Fig. 69). The thick wall of the façade was displaced by several meters to enlarge the first hypostyle hall and make room for twenty-four columns instead of the original sixteen. The central

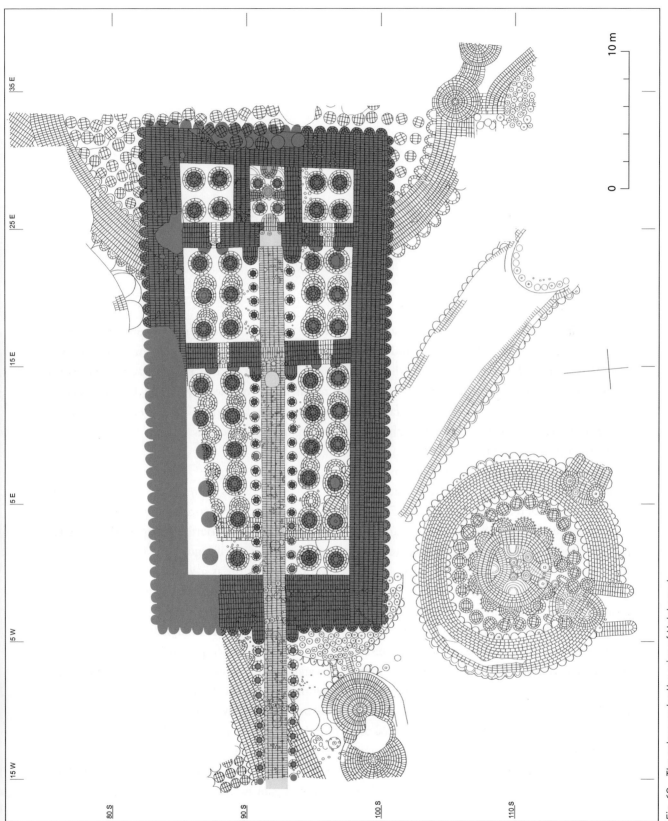

Fig. 69　The palace under the reign of Hatshepsut

aisle was also flanked by colonnades that continued into the interior of the palace. A first, and slight, closing system has been identified, but the main entry into the palace was located in a veritable pylon. It was furnished with the usual pivots and a fastening device, restored twice. A second door on the same alignment opened into the second hypostyle hall; there, too, the number of columns was increased, this time from eight to twelve. Two side doors facilitated movement between the hypostyle halls (Fig. 70).

The throne room was flanked by two annexes, each with four columns and each with its own door. In the center of the throne room, a single step led into a space almost entirely occupied by a round offering table of African type, surrounded by three seats. The four large column bases of a canopy must have impeded movement inside the room. A rounded two-step staircase preceded the throne, located on the axis. The side colonnades of the central aisle continued to the entrance of the throne room. Familiar Egyptian models must certainly have influenced this harmonious plan, which preserved the dimensions of the previous monument while lengthening the building. Only the throne room itself is not compa-

rable to Pharaonic examples: we are left with the unmistakable impression that the architectural style of oval or circular palaces was adapted to the requirements of the *mnnw,* and that Hatshepsut preserved the layout conceived by her father when enlarging the palace.

THE SECOND *MNNW*

Even though our evidence is limited to the ceremonial precinct and the northern front of the outer fortifications, we can recognize the importance of the *mnnw* institution as a whole, which required an unprecedented construction effort. When reconstructed in its entirety, the bastioned enclosure with its extraordinary gates occupied a considerable surface. We must not forget that the Nubian and African cities that dominated the region menaced the south flank of the Egyptian Empire. Dukki Gel demonstrates how the strong and independent Kingdom of Kerma and its allies became a regional force that also had an impact on Central Africa. Once the frontier of the Second Cataract was secured, Egypt was able to focus on controlling the

supply of goods vital to the empire's development. These enemy lands had been able to extend their military might, but step by step the Egyptian sovereigns prepared to conquer them (Monnier 2010, 117–164).

Establishing the *mnnw* was part of this conquest and is evidence of the considerable investment necessary to overcome violent resistance. The overall infrastructure, with its enormous defensive system, was constructed in response to a very real threat. The inhabitants of these regions benefited from attack strategies and unusual defensive systems that were perhaps unfamiliar to the Egyptian armies, and the military installations of previously unknown type that we have discovered must certainly have changed the rules of war. Most notable was the influ-

ence of defensive techniques that did not belong to the Egyptian tradition, such as bastioned enclosures and fortified gates. We do not know to what extent the local populace played a determining role in these conflicts, and demographic studies are just beginning for the periods in question. What we do know is that the reconquest by a native coalition was part of a prolonged conflict and explains the considerable efforts undertaken by Thutmose II and Hatshepsut. The reconstruction of the *mnnw* is impressive evidence of the decision to maintain the cult buildings and restore the surrounding fortifications. Although the sanctuaries themselves continued to be constructed of mudbrick, the use of stone for the pillars of the hypostyle halls required the opening of quarries far from Dukki Gel. The fortifications, of colossal proportions, were designed to convey to Nubians and Africans that resistance was futile. The northwest foregate was, without any doubt, one of the strong points of the new defensive system, and the hypostyle halls at the north end of the gate must have been built with the welcome of important visitors in mind. Rules of interaction with the local population no doubt evolved as a hierarchy was developed. Ceremonial passages were flanked by colonnades, emphasizing the importance of processions. The ensemble as a whole seems designed to reflect a grandiose image of Egypt.

Occupation of the Territory by Thutmose III

In the twenty-second year of the reign of Thutmose III, Queen Hatshepsut disappeared and the king alone controlled the fate of the empire. He organized at least fourteen military campaigns into Asia, while Nubia itself did not seem to be troublesome (Vandersleyen 1995, 308–312). It was only at the end of his reign, after several decades had passed, that he undertook a campaign to the land of Kush. In Dukki Gel, archaeological remains reveal a city completely transformed: the enclosure was simplified, with a wall fortified in places by small redans. The walled area was apparently extended to the north (Fig. 71), where we are unable to excavate due to the presence of a farm. Farther away, 400 meters beyond the walls, we found a quadrangular building aligned almost exactly with the dromos of the transformed central temple. Thus it appears that the city was greatly expanded and its external fortifications eliminated. Thutmose III had no fear of rebellion, as the countryside seemed to have been pacified (Morkot 2000, 69–90).

The king's architectural program was considerable, as both palaces and temples were entirely rebuilt. The use of stone increased considerably. But what is even more significant in this period is the systematic dismantling of the monuments of Hatshepsut. The pillars of the hypostyle halls were pulled down and their sandstone blocks, decorated in rich relief, reduced to small fragments; rarely are these decorative elements preserved. The west temple was abandoned, although part of its hypostyle hall was preserved as a transverse chapel providing access to the central temple. This chapel is on the axis of two temples constructed on the location of earlier cult buildings. The same transverse axis continued into an oblong space between the temples, possibly a series of annexes belonging to an institution similar to the "House of Gold," the place where statues came to life, a place of consecration also used for the care of liturgical objects.

The enclosure wall turned to the north, following a wall that defined the original area of the native religious precinct to the northeast. An entry along the extended transverse axis provided access to this earlier place of worship, maintained outside the city walls. With the addition of connecting bastions, surveillance of the native complex was ensured. After skirting the African quarter, the wall turned once again and continued north. The layout maintained the two

0   20 m

50.00N   50 .00N

0.00   0 .00

50.00S   50.00S

100.00S   100.00S

150.00S   150.00S

200.00S   200.00S

Fig. 71 Schematic plan of Dukki Gel during the
reign of Thutmose III

African cult structures outside the city while allowing a strict watch over them. These walls were not all built at the same time: the fortifications north of the native quarter were constructed in two successive phases. We may well ask ourselves why it was necessary to erect a gate limiting access to the native places of worship and increase the fortifications in this area.

As we could observe, the enclosure of Thutmose III underwent modifications. South of the central temple, bastions were constructed directly against the sanctuary wall. These defenses were poorly anchored in the ground, as if they were built not to last but instead to provide a short-term addition to the fortifications. As we can see from the abundant ceramic material, the construction work undertaken during the long reign of Thutmose III was vital to the resupply of ancient Pnubs. As well as the reconstruction of the two temples and a palace, many other parts of the city probably remain to be discovered.

FORTIFICATIONS

Three circular pits were uncovered at the western edge of the fortifications along the line of the enclosure attributed to the reign of Thutmose III. The pit deposits yielded several hundred potsherds dating to the early Eighteenth Dynasty. As yet poorly understood, this sector may represent the remains of a ritual associated with the building of an enclosure that continued to the west, where the city limits have not yet been located. These three deposits are comparable to circular pits 0.60 meters in diameter dug into the destruction levels of a bastion constructed by the Nubian or African coalitions. The ceramic material includes large numbers of beer vessels and bread molds for offerings. These remains may be contemporary with the reign of Thutmose III, as the refuse inventoried from the first stratigraphic levels yielded numerous seal impressions dating to the New Kingdom. This fortified line in front of the east temple was probably abandoned under Hatshepsut.

The enclosure of Thutmose III was erected in several phases, its masonry varying in thickness as construction proceeded. In a deep sounding along the west wall parallel to the temples, we found an older foundation wall 1.20 meters wide. Subsequently redans with the same dimension, 1.20 meters, were added to this wall. The redans were scaled down and adapted to the thickness of the wall, very different from the massive Nubian enclosures of the New Kingdom, such as those at Sesebi or Soleb. Still later, the enclosure wall of Dukki Gel was enlarged to 2.40 meters in width and other bastions added. Near the northeast religious precinct, the wall was strengthened with massive connected bastions. As we have seen, the ensemble was quite irregular. Originally the enclosure was oriented askew; later it was redrawn along a more orthogonal line.

EGYPTIAN TEMPLES AND NATIVE PLACES OF WORSHIP

The central temple was completely reworked after the almost complete leveling of the west temple. The grand hypostyle hall of the entrance was also dismantled. The dromos, on the other hand, was given priority and a side avenue added to join the road from the reconstructed northeast palace. Probably at the same time, a well was dug into this avenue in front of the central temple, whose elongated foundations are preserved in a first course of enormous sandstone blocks. The temple doorway was also constructed of stone. A fairly narrow pylon may have existed on either side of the entrance, where extensive remnants of mudbrick masonry were found. The line of the side walls of the temple was followed to a new southern limit, forming the corner of the building beyond the sanctuary.

Construction in this area was undertaken in several stages, and we have found some indication that a measurement system was used. When constructing their massive complexes and walls, Hatshepsut's master builders had to take into account, at the south end of the temple, the fortifications of the religious precinct. The staircase and underground passage down to the water level of the well also complicated construction and had to be considered. Thus the building program of Thutmose III required a certain reorganization while preserving features that were essential to the whole. Large round pits were dug into the ruined masses of masonry. The pits were probably dug to repair previous foundations, and parallelepiped blocks were placed on the bottom as alignment reference points. The southeast corner of the building was marked with the abandoned line of a staircase through the fortification wall to the south, where another architectural group is associated with the staircase for obtaining sacred water. These reference points must also have been used to calculate height.

Mudbrick foundations, which appear to have been laid out in circles, have not been excavated to any depth. These concentric circles may have served as foundation deposits since we found, on the surface of one of the older examples, a piece of gold leaf bearing the impression of two ears; another deposit comprised miniature bricks of sandstone wrapped in gold leaf. The southeast corner of the central temple was also underlined by a circle of this type. In all likelihood this impressive south wall was constructed over the staircase leading to the well, but access was still provided by the underground passage to the north, while some complicated modifications converted the passage designed for the earlier west temple.

Returning to the description of the main temple: its entrance led to a vast courtyard partially covered by a light roof that protected two porticos on either side of a central aisle. Small column bases probably supported wooden shafts. In front of a door

constructed on top of the dismantled pillars of the peripteral portico, a pavement of large, very thick flagstones measuring 3.50 meters to a side was installed. This podium must have served a ceremonial purpose for worshippers entering the hypostyle hall. Construction of the hall required considerable effort to stabilize robust pillars supporting a stone roof; the foundation trenches are more than 1 meter deep. They consist of four parallel excavations with cross trenches. Thus we can reconstruct four rows of three pillars, with one of the enormous circular bases upended in the destruction levels (Fig. 72). This considerable weight was resting on a thick layer of sifted yellow sand, where we also found a course of large, very regular gray sandstone blocks incised with architect's marks representing part of the structure.

Three side doors led into the hypostyle hall. In the easternmost entrance, the semicircular courses of the wall foundation were visible next to the doorposts. A very long threshold, consisting of a double row of worn sandstone blocks, extended between the mudbrick door frames. A stone podium was located outside the door, next to the temenos

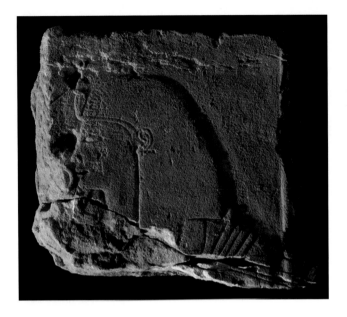

Fig. 72 Decorated stone block from a pillar in the hypostyle hall: Thutmose III

opening into a neighboring temple. On the other side, to the west, a door restored during the Amarna Period led into a chapel that reused parts of the west temple of Hatshepsut, including several pillars from the hypostyle hall and a segment of the peripteral portico. Farther south, we were able to reconstruct a third door from the massive foundations of the doorposts and a central passage. In the layers corresponding to the door opening, we found decorated blocks with the cartouche of Thutmose III and fragmentary texts from a doorpost.

There was no change in the plan of the tripartite sanctuary and its pronaos. Only the fourth annex, used to access the stairs down to the well, was modified to create a new access point incorporating the underground corridor of the disused west temple. A thick rounded wall constricted the stairwell leading from a door of the annex to the middle of the underground corridor. Two steps of the stone staircase were still in situ. Considerable labor was required to improve access from the hypostyle hall to the well. The side wall of the temple was rectilinear, and the annex was extended to the north to serve as a vestibule before the entrance to the hypostyle hall. These

structural modifications took into account access to the water table and created a more monumental passage after the abandonment of the south staircase.

The terrain recuperated to the west made room for the workshops to expand; a large rectangular oven, heavily reddened by fire, was added to the area. The residential precinct remained in use and expanded to the south. The south end of the east temple was completely transformed. The dismantled hypostyle hall was reconstructed on top of the sandstone fragments of Hatshepsut's carefully leveled pillars. The large circular mudbrick foundation of the central pillar was found in good condition, and five rows of five columns of the hypostyle hall have been uncovered. The side walls turn the corner at their southern end along a new alignment, defined by two brick circles preserved in the corners. The sanctuary must have been enlarged and its interior reworked, although no trace of its interior organization has been preserved. The brick circles at the southwest and southeast corners yielded, respectively, two small uninscribed sandstone bricks wrapped in gold leaf and a sherd bearing the name of Thutmose III.

A CEREMONIAL PALACE

Hatshepsut's palace was abandoned and, immediately to the north, another palace was constructed during the reign of Thutmose III. The plan of this building was established along an oblique axis that continued through a wide passage turning along the dromos and ending in front of the entrance to the central temple (Fig. 73). We cannot provide specific dates for this complicated area without an in-depth chronological study, but we do know that New Kingdom potsherds are associated with its development. We were able to ascertain that a pavement of sandstone slabs led from the palace toward the temple. The stones were partially removed, but in the center some of them preserved their original alignment in the direction of the entrance to the east temple. The pavement was then modified to continue to the west. The paving stones were perfectly joined and can be compared to aisles at Gebel Barkal. Low walls must have originally flanked this processional way, whose pavement continued inside a large gate. This entrance in front of the palace was made of stone, mostly reused. Carefully constructed,

the gate was 11 meters long. A foundation trench had a layer of fine sand with three courses of bricks for a peripheral retaining wall and blocks of stone. The two doorposts were also of stone. Such a monumental entrance may have functioned as a window of appearance (a ceremonial window where the king appeared on different occasions), while around and behind it an apartment was provided for the sovereign to prepare for procession. Above the levels of the sizable stone fragments from the door, the mud-brick building was rectangular in plan, with a reception hall and an annex behind. Only the south side of the central part of the building is still preserved. It consists of several irregular rooms accessible through a small concealed opening. This palace underwent several subsequent transformations, and the presence of fired bricks is proof that the building was still in use during the Meroitic Period, 1,000 years later.

THE ANCIENT CITY OF PNUBS, PACIFIED

Judging from the new configuration of the city, the king had it under his control. The native religious precinct, reduced to two places of worship, was

Fig. 73   The restored palace next to the palace of Hatshepsut

maintained to the northeast. The urban area extended to the north, but we have little information on its spread and do not know if other defensive lines were established along the earlier fortified fronts. In his Annals at Karnak, Thutmose III reported that the land of Kush paid regular tribute to Egypt, and it was only at the end of his reign that he conducted one last military campaign in Nubia. So for several decades the region lived in peace, as the remains of the city center seem to indicate (Vandersleyen 1995, 294–308).

Remains of Thutmose IV at Pnubs

After the long reign of Amenhotep II, about which we know almost nothing at the site of Dukki Gel apart from a fragment of door lintel, the accession to the throne of Thutmose IV begins another page in the long history of ancient Pnubs. We may think that the nine-year reign of this Pharaoh profited from a period of calm (Vandersleyen 1995, 343–359); it is therefore interesting to note that the sanctuary of the central temple was rebuilt in stone, and construction work under the authority of the Pharaoh also took place at Gebel Barkal (Fig. 74). The two military expeditions undertaken to Nubia were minor frontier interventions. Thus it is hardly surprising that the city that Thutmose III completely transformed remained unchanged for quite a long time. We must, however, note that structural remains are few and therefore give us an inaccurate idea of the buildings.

In the sanctuary of the central temple, evidence for the building works of Thutmose IV is provided by three foundation deposits (Fig. 75). Two were located in the southern corners of the temple and the third in a circular pit northeast of the pronaos. These deposits consisted of several dozen small faience plaques with the name of Thutmose IV, three with the name of Thutmose III, and thirty to fifty miniature vessels of brown clay as well as faience necklaces of tubular and circular beads. Each of the three circular pits contained layers of sand and wet soil below the first course of sandstone blocks, upon whose surface construction lines were sometimes visible. A corridor that provided access to side rooms preceded the tripartite sanctuary. A pronaos, connected to the hypostyle hall of Thutmose III, was preserved in place.

The palace probably kept its original plan, and the avenue that turned toward the main temple followed the same route. The dromos continued to the north, where we excavated an axial well, carefully built of regular stone blocks. Beginning in the reign of Thutmose III, an enclosure surrounded this well on three sides. We did not locate a wall on the south side, but uncovered in this area several small sandstone basins that must have belonged to private cults. Aligned more or less along the dromos and the slope of the elevated causeway in this sector of the city, the basins are rectangular in shape except for one circular example. Dominating this ensemble was a large vat sitting on a layer of irregular stone slabs

Fig. 74 Schematic plan of Dukki Gel
during the reign of Thutmose IV

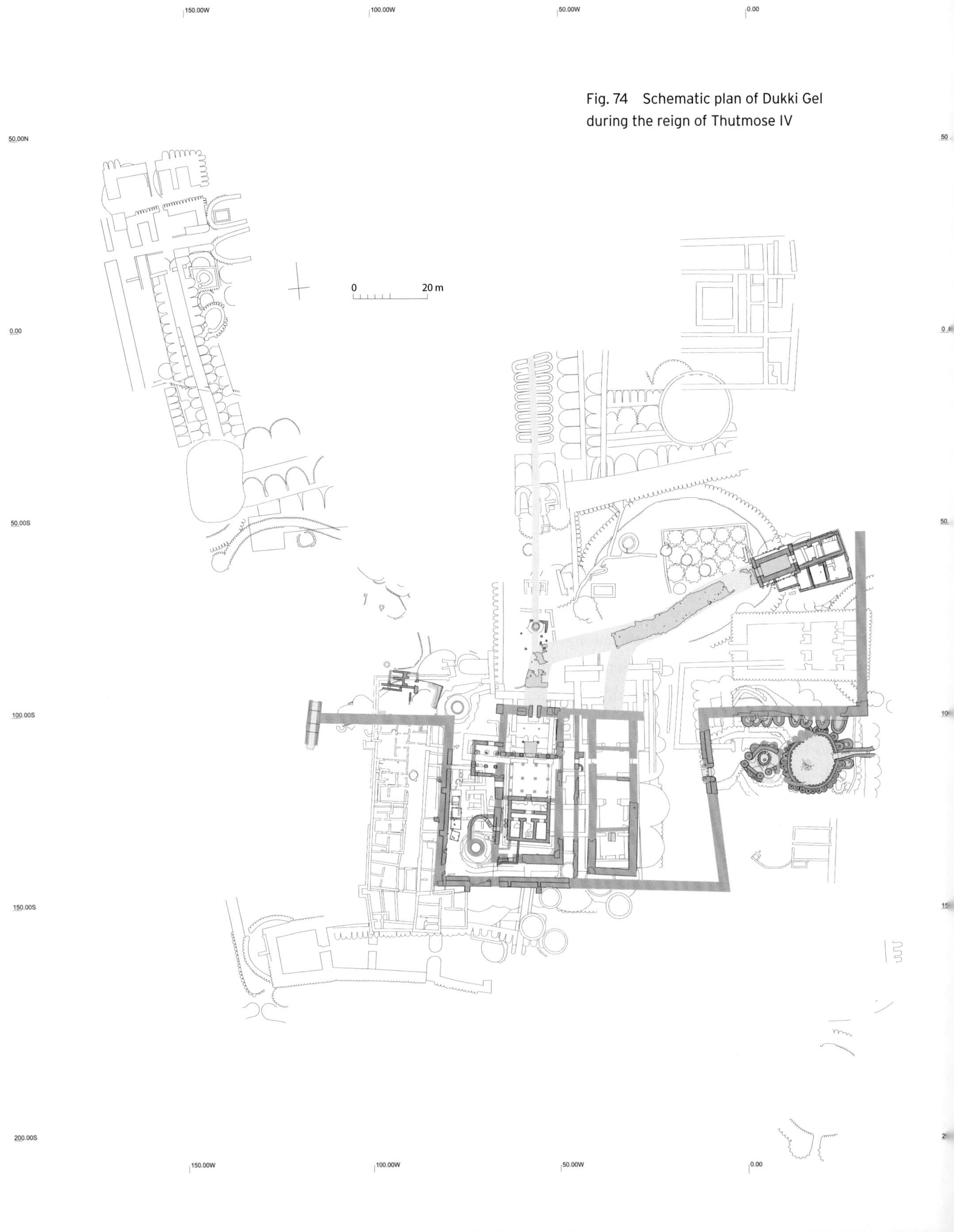

150.00W   100.00W   50.00W   0.00

50.00N

0.00

50.00S

100.00S

150.00S

200.00S

0   20 m

150.00W   100.00W   50.00W   0.00

Fig. 75   A foundation deposit beneath the sanctuary of Thutmose IV

directly in line with the causeway. These religious in-stallations, frequented by the common folk, belonged to long-lived cults, if we are to judge by the super-imposition of water-related features that were quite flimsy in themselves but nevertheless required the installation of a substantial pavement.

Equally noteworthy, next to the stairwell leading to the water table of the south well, is the presence of a rectilinear wall that changed the alignment of the ramp. This modification was related to a large-scale reorganization of the open area that extended from the western side gate to the hypostyle hall of Thutmose III. These construction works were asso-ciated with the creation of a substantial storage area probably meant for grain. On the same level we found an impressive layer of large, crudely hewn blocks of hard stone. By analogy with other rectan-gular silos typical of the region, we can reconstruct on this stone base a superstructure of almost square wooden storerooms, probably reserved for the prep-aration of sanctuary offerings. A workshop belonging

to preceding phases continued in use, and we can conclude that the remains to the west of this area, including bread molds and cattle bones, are evi-dence of cult activity.

Most likely the temple sanctuary remained in use, despite its mudbrick walls, since the foundation of the *mnnw,* because not a single structural stone block was found in this area predating Thutmose IV. During his reign, however, sturdy foundations supported walls decorated with very fine bas-reliefs. Several sandstone fragments were inventoried in the destruc-tion layers of the sanctuary. The east temple suffered greatly from Amarna and Meroitic destructions, making it impossible to identify a contemporary phase in the southern part of the temple, which was completely destroyed down to the foundations of Thutmose I. The stratigraphy in the center of the hy-postyle hall does, however, reveal several construction phases that preceded the building program of Amen-hotep IV / Akhenaten. Indeed, the remnants of sub-stantial walls remain to be interpreted.

The Amarna Reform

The Amarna episode is well known in Egypt. At this time many cult buildings were destroyed and then rapidly reconstructed by the envoys of the heretic Pharaoh (Kemp 2012). Not far from Dukki Gel, the site of Sesebi (Laboury 2010, 386–387 nn. 137–138) allows us to consider a city and the two temples founded by Amenhotep IV, who in his fourth year took the name Akhenaten for the remaining thirteen years of his reign. The situation at Dukki Gel is, however, exceptional: the two Thutmosid temples were torn down to their foundations and reconstructed according to plans influenced by the Amarna reforms, including the use of talatat, standardized building blocks measuring 0.52 by 0.22 by 0.18 meters and easily carried by a single man (Fig. 76). Subsequently the accomplishments of the Amarna Period were almost completely obliterated, probably under Seti I. Thus we are able to study the transformation of the site during a very short time frame and note the violent destruction carried out during the reform.

All the building activity, which was considerable, was concentrated on the places of worship and most certainly involved an important investment of skilled labor. It is quite extraordinary that these efforts were undertaken so far from the recently founded capital of Tell el-Amarna, especially when we take into consideration other sites in the region such as Sesebi and Gebel Barkal (Kendall 2009, 2–16). All of Nubia was thus affected by this revolution. The Pnubs enclosure may have been reinforced with a thick exterior face, but we do not have absolute proof of this fact. The paved avenue to the palace was probably restored, as we can distinguish a second level of slabs before the entry to the main temple. Moreover, the door itself was radically transformed, which required modifications to the dromos and the causeway to the east.

THE MAIN TEMPLE DEDICATED TO ATEN

The central Thutmosid temple suffered systematic destruction, as evidenced by a thick layer of sandstone fragments. Blocks belonging to earlier structures were nevertheless recuperated and reworked. In fact, some of the talatat had on one of their sides the remnants of previous bas-relief decoration. Some column bases and foundations bore cut marks from

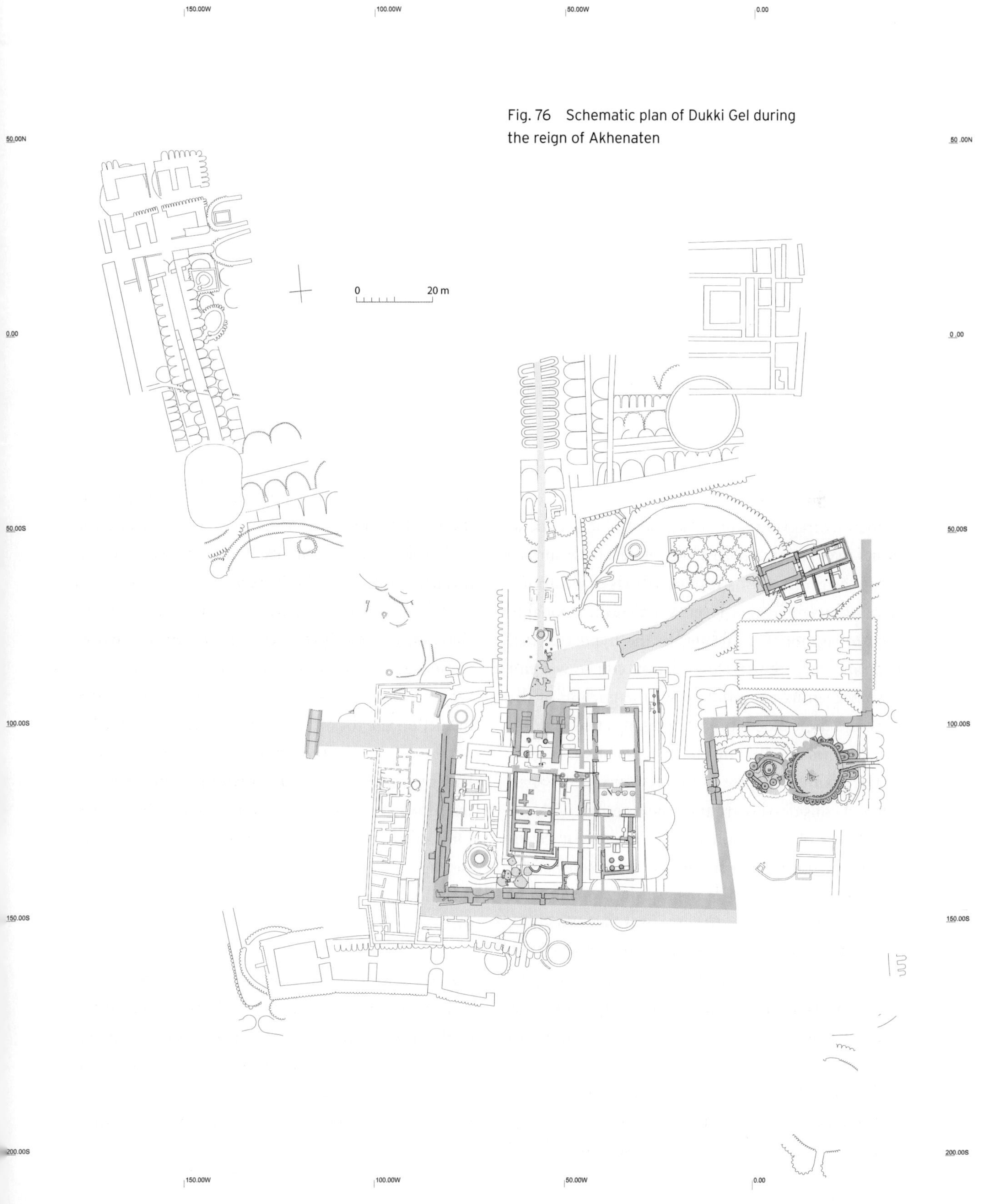

Fig. 76 Schematic plan of Dukki Gel during the reign of Akhenaten

0   20 m

Fig. 77   The central temple, destroyed during the Amarna Period

destruction. In the rubble layer, we also noted numerous fragments of abandoned blocks and, in places, wet layers, perhaps used to level the surface before beginning construction. Rows of postholes were observed in this layer; stakes were probably used to support scaffolding. In the hypostyle hall and sanctuary, the first foundation course was not recovered in its entirety; during the gutting of the structure these blocks probably disappeared beneath the accumulation of sandstone fragments (Fig. 77).

The plan of the gate of the new temple of Aten differed considerably from its predecessors with the narrowing of the pylon moles. The architect increased the monumental aspect of both sides of the gate by transforming the pylon into a simpler but more massive entrance (Bonnet and Valbelle 2007, 55–63). This was a characteristic feature of openings, as represented on the bas-reliefs and plans preserved at Amarna (Kemp 2012, 88–91). However, the presence or absence of a pylon with stone masonry for the door and brick additions remains an open question at Dukki Gel. Indeed, we have found a row of talatat lining the doorway, which had on its west side massive brick constructions measuring

8 by 7 meters. It is possible that this brickwork was supplemented by a wall that has not survived. The architecture of the capital at Tell el-Amarna exhibits multiple aspects, and entryways differ one from another (for example, Laboury 2010, 165–168).

In the courtyard following the entry, a platform composed of a layer of talatat emphasized and prolonged the threshold. The same system was found inside, on the location of the former hypostyle hall of Thutmose III. The Amarna courtyard probably had two side porticos whose four stone columns rested on large rounded foundations of mudbrick. One of the column bases still in situ was constructed of two half-columns of brown sandstone, a technique that facilitated transport. To make room for a transverse passage leading to the chapel on the west and a major passage on the east, the south wall was moved slightly more than 1 meter farther south, resulting in an almost square courtyard. One of the uprights of a side door is partially preserved, as are paving stones leading to the chapel. The chapel itself underwent numerous transformations, and its remains from the reign of Akhenaten have disappeared.

The hypostyle hall was leveled; only the first course of wall was partially preserved. A thick layer of sandstone fragments covered the entire surface. A few talatat remain in situ on the rubble, including several from the platform next to the north entrance and a few rare blocks from the east wall, as well as the foundations of structures that replaced the foundations of the room. Although evidence is lacking, we can envisage a newly reorganized space, perhaps to hold a series of pedestals for offering tables. The remains are not extensive enough to determine if the platform was related to an axial passage or if these few talatat were actual pedestals, as was the case in the "Long Temple in the enclosure of the Great Aten Temple" (Kemp 2012, 89–93).

The south wall of the former hypostyle hall was also modified. Its thickness was reduced and several pilasters added to its south face. These pilasters may be related to a series of storage areas in a long room preceding the pronaos. It was necessary to pass through this room to reach the sanctuary, whose stone architecture dates to the reign of Thutmose IV. Starting with the pronaos, talatat, secured with great quantities of gypsum, replaced block masonry. In the tripartite sanctuary and the pronaos, pavements were surfaced with a covering of reused stone slabs, while talatat were used principally for wall construction. These restorations preserved the layout of the former sanctuary, whose proportions remained almost identical. Thus post-destruction reconstruction essentially proceeded along the former plan. Some of the foundations of Thutmose IV were leveled horizontally to provide a base for a thick layer of gypsum securing the first course of talatat (Bonnet 2001, 205–210).

Beneath the southeast side door of the entrance courtyard were the remains of two foundation deposits, thus serving to emphasize the importance of the transverse passage. The deposit beneath the north doorpost was located directly under the first course of stone that had been worked to some extent. Removal of the west and south faces of the mudbrick wall mass revealed jars crushed by its weight. On the other side of the entrance, the deposit was located behind the doorpost. There two jars were preserved in situ, while a small alabaster cup in the shape of a duck was placed nearby. An almost illegible baked clay seal and ceramic cups were encircled by sandstone fragments (Bonnet 2003, 264–266). Beyond this door the passage was lined with mudbrick columns very close to the walls. These columns were found on the south side of the passage only but must also have existed along the north wall, by analogy to similar layouts from the late New Kingdom and the Napatan Period.

The column foundations were of mudbrick arranged in superimposed circular courses in a very regular pattern. A central beam left a square impression that can be traced from one course to the next. We do not know if these bases supported a stone superstructure, but we did find very fine layers of gypsum at different levels in the courses of brick. Such was also the case for the massive mudbrick structure of the grand entrance to the temple, where some masonry joins were emphasized by vertical and horizontal lines of white. The shafts of the three columns of the transverse portico must have measured from 0.80 to 0.90 meters in diameter: the centers of their bases are imprinted with this dimension, while the bases themselves were more than 1.60 meters in diameter. Along this row of column bases, several reused blocks were aligned to form a fairly deep channel. Two of these blocks are nicely decorated with the head of Thutmose III.

The central portico with its transverse passage must have joined a wall to the south because another column base is located next to a door leading in that direction, while a thick wall separated the annexes of the two temples. This area was destroyed by later construction, most notably an installation associated with a bronze workshop as yet unexcavated. A stone doorway off the transverse passage faced the east temple; this axis must have continued through the building, as indicated by breaches in the brick foundations of the east wall. These foundations were partially identified next to the sanctuary established after the Amarna revolution, but these levels have greatly suffered from later construction, especially the restorations following the reign of Akhenaten. Let us also note that the north part of the structure is covered by the remains of Napatan and Meroitic temples, which soundings in this area would have endangered.

The temple plan is remarkable, as south of the transverse passage, a door with a platform was aligned along the main axis, forming perhaps an alleyway, and opened onto a portico and a vast courtyard. A channel at an oblique angle cut through the circular brick base of one of the columns. A second courtyard occupied a narrower space in the main part of the cult building. This courtyard was aligned along the temple axis, although a rather peculiar side door was located on the east side. A porch with a roof supported by two columns preceded the door. The doorway, with two rounded doorposts and a wood floor, was unusual, and a thick wall reinforced this feature. What we would consider to be the sanc-

tuary was contained within solid walls laid out in an irregular plan. A large pit was dug into the temple axis and, toward the back of the complex, four columns completed the ensemble, which was probably partially roofed. Additional structures, destroyed now, were located behind the south wall.

Although a number of small premises may have been added to this sanctuary, we are still able to compare its plan to the three sanctuaries with four columns each from the temple of Sesebi, dating to the first year of the reign of Amenhotep IV (Laboury 2010, 113–114). This fortified city, a neighbor of Pnubs, certainly had close connections with the entire region, including Kawa (the ancient Gematon), as well as Gebel Barkal and Napata. But to continue with the analysis of the structures uncovered around the temples of Dukki Gel during the Amarna Period, we note a section of wall behind the sanctuary of the east temple. Around the south part of the neighboring main temple, we found a wall that may have surrounded the entire building, perhaps a temenos that separated the sacred area from the workshops on the south side, along with their

Fig. 78   The floor of the east temple paved with reused talatat

Fig. 79   Talatat in the Dukki Gel storeroom

circular silos with small buttresses and an open area for preparing temple offerings. An abundance of cylindrical bread molds confirms this activity. A nearby chapel may have held a special meaning for the artisans in these workshops.

In the Napatan temple to the east, we uncovered a floor constructed with talatat (Fig. 78). These blocks were decorated and provide an excellent opportunity to compare the iconography of scenes from Dukki Gel with those of the main sites from the reign of Akhenaten (Valbelle 1999, 84, 85; 2001, 230, 233; 2003, 291–292). Our talatat, however, were not in their original location, and there is no indication that they were associated with the stone masonry in the east temple. We note the absence of gypsum fragments or stone foundations in the levels comparable to the temple. We must also note that at Sesebi talatat were not in use under Amenhotep IV before he began his reign as Akhenaten. Thus we propose that the east temple was contemporary with the earlier years of this pharaoh and the talatat came from the neighboring temple (Fig. 79).

The Ramesside Occupation

The destructions in the city of Pnubs–Dukki Gel probably took place under the command of Seti I (Masquelier-Loorius 2013, 95–109, 142–154), and certain reconstructions can be dated to his reign by a few inscribed blocks. The remains of this period are sparse; only the column bases located in the entry courtyard of the central temple belong to this building program. There we found talatat reused in foundations as well as the reused halves of column shafts. Considerable building activity took place in the native religious precinct in the northeast, where a single circular sanctuary replaced the oval places of worship. In the direct vicinity, postholes and ceramic deposits provide evidence of ceremonial activity. We may be dealing with the construction of circular buildings in wood, a feature that developed little by little in front of the religious monument until the Napatan Period. The Ramesside levels were completely rebuilt, so following the layout of the contemporaneous postholes of a given period is particularly difficult.

The religious building was restored in a strange way. An exterior wall was surrounded and reinforced by connected bastions. The west door led into a hypostyle hall with *galous* columns 1 meter in diameter. There were dozens of these earthen circles, leaving us to conclude that the bases had been reused several times. They were arranged either along an interior circle or in a more irregular pattern. Shallowly sunk into the soil, these foundations could not have provided sufficient support for the heavy superstructures, which explains the numerous episodes of rebuilding. A rounded wooden vestibule must have preceded the entrance. The native inhabitants thus regained a certain amount of power in the northeast quarter of the city, and their place of worship retained its influence through the long upheavals that followed the Ramesside Period.

The end of the Egyptian occupation in Nubia is poorly documented. The current state of research does not allow us to determine with any precision either historical phases or population movements, and ancient Pnubs certainly falls within this gap in our knowledge. The stratigraphy in front of the central Egyptian temple has yielded numerous impressions from the sealing of doors and vessels. While the reigns of the Eighteenth Dynasty are extensively represented, we have little information about later periods apart from a fragmentary stela of Ramesses II found in a pit, to which we may add a few rare documents from the end of the New Kingdom. The enormous dunes that formed over the site during the Ramesside and Early Napatan Periods may be the result of an as yet unexplained climatic change. Environmental degradation may well have led to a shift in the way of life of the inhabitants.

The Kushite Kingship

The Twenty-Fifth Dynasty in Egypt corresponded to a renaissance in Nubia (Kendall 2014, 663–686). Although the great Napatan Pharaohs controlled the length of the Nile Valley, their roots remained firmly in the region between the Third and Fourth Cataracts, the ancient territory of the Kingdom of Kerma. The Egyptianization of Nubian society acted as a unifying force, led by the ruling class. It is interesting to observe how this phenomenon evolved in stages. While funerary customs changed quite suddenly for the elite classes, for example, the transformation was much more gradual for the population as a whole (Bonnet 1999b, 251–256; 1995, 50–52). Domestic architecture also changed, with Egyptian influence slowly making its mark from the seventh century BCE on (Mohamed Ahmed 1992, 33–73, figs. 3 and 4). Further study of the transition that took place around 1000 BCE is necessary to fully understand the phases of occupation.

Profound transformations occurred at Dukki Gel during this period, but since the temples were constantly reconstructed, few traces of the Kushite Period remain (Bonnet and Valbelle 2007, 64–69). Two large blocks are inscribed with the cartouche of Pharaoh Shabaka. Judging by the proportions of these blocks, Shabaka must have been responsible for an important monument, but his building stones were reused for the pylon foundation of the Napatan east temple. It is thus not possible to determine the location of Shabaka's buildings. We also do not know who built the east chapel adjoining the sanctuary of the central temple. Both the large foundation blocks and the sandstone used in the temple are very fine indeed. The quality of these materials and the method of dressing in the quarry invite comparison with those of the temple of Taharqa at Tabo. The parallel lines of bands sculpted at an angle are fairly characteristic, as is the poor quality of the brown and yellow sandstone, which could disintegrate into powder. Moreover, two pedestals of a granite naos with cornice were found overturned, one in the sanctuary of the east temple and the other in the main axis of this temple in front of the chapel, and were almost identical to the one installed under Taharqa in Monument B500 at Gebel Barkal (Fig. 80).

The chapel, 10 meters in length, provided a connection between the two temples, which continued

to follow the New Kingdom plan. The chapel opened to the east. Its fragmentary pavement outlined an entrance platform with four columns whose drums were recovered from the debris. It is also possible to situate the altar from the pattern of the pavement that surrounded it. Several bronze furnaces were preserved behind the small sanctuary on the north side. Based on a type normally used for baking bread, these furnaces appear to have been adapted to yield much higher temperatures. Air conduits provided ventilation. The furnaces were constructed of large, slightly tapered sections of ceramic, with extremely thick, heavily burnt walls.

Fig. 80   A side chapel of the Twenty-Fifth Dynasty restored in the Meroitic Period

The Napatan Kingdom

The rulers at the beginning of the Napatan Period considered themselves the overlords of Egypt, but the Saite Pharaohs were able to regain power. There were serious conflicts in Nubia until the expedition of Psammetichus II, who destroyed several cities in the region (Bonnet and Valbelle 2007, 155–171). Pnubs did not escape the devastation, and the armies of Kush, led by King Aspelta, took refuge farther south. From the archaeological point of view, this destruction allowed us to identify badly burnt levels and understand how the principal structures of Dukki Gel were destroyed and later rebuilt. Upon the death of Psammetichus II, Aspelta was able to begin a sizable building program. Although rebuilt in more modest proportions with simpler decoration, the temples regained some of their splendor. Apart from Dukki Gel, fragments of toppled statues of ancestral kings were collected and hidden in caches at Gebel Barkal, and more recently in Dangeil (Bonnet and Valbelle 2007) (Fig. 81). The orientation of the dromos associated with the reconstructed main temple remained the same in the northern part of the site. The well in its path was restored with a new coping of large slabs and a narrower

enclosure wall. In front of the well, a "fire altar" was installed in the center of a structure supported by two small annexes containing ceramic offering vessels embedded in brick. An early Napatan jar was discovered in situ. This entire installation was covered in lime wash, still clearly visible. A circular base completed the ensemble to the south. After a detailed examination of the solid mass of the altar, we were surprised to discover the remnants of an indigenous door and two adjoining towers. The line of the dromos was thus preserved for a considerable time, and the master builders were completely familiar with the architectural traditions of the past.

The main temple appears to have followed the plan of its predecessors, although the first courtyard was open to the north, perhaps to make room for the royal statues certainly located just at the entrance. To the east, enormous walls must reflect the layout later reused for the cache of the statues. The four supports of the courtyard, with its two porticos, were preserved in the south, and the side door on the west side led into the completely reconstructed side chapel. The lower courses of the walls

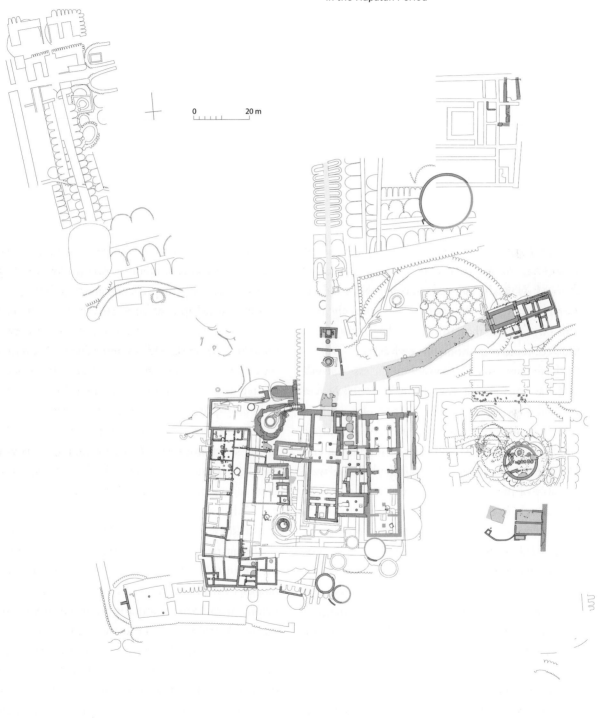

Fig. 81   Schematic plan of Dukki Gel
in the Napatan Period

were constructed of reused structural blocks alternating with brick masonry. *Opus africanum* comes to mind, which in our case considerably predates Roman examples. The masonry was heavily reddened by fire, and the destroyed building was reconstructed, more conventionally, with brick.

The entrance to the courtyard on the east side still used the transverse passage originally established in the New Kingdom. The passage was prolonged by a porticoed aisle up to and through the east temple. The hypostyle hall and sanctuary of the central cult building are poorly preserved, but the columns were probably of brick and the sanctuary itself tripartite. Immediately to the west, two residences with associated multi-unit outbuildings covered a considerable surface. This area, located close to the two wells, was used for the preparation of bread, beer, and meat offerings in the neighboring sanctuaries. The two residences were reserved for important individuals in charge of the institutions. Given the numerous rooms and kitchens in these houses, they must also have hosted receptions. Perhaps the priests themselves lived there.

The work units of the outbuildings were arranged around a courtyard where numerous bread ovens and an ash box were found. Superimposed levels indicate a very long period of use. Some of these units were reserved for the preparation of meat, as indicated by thick layers of bone. According to analysis by Louis Chaix, the bones belonged to young cattle. Other rooms, probably occupied by the administration, were connected to each unit. A corridor, located at the end of a long courtyard serving the workshops, led to the north well, thus providing convenient access to water. A bit farther away, next to the sanctuaries, enormous circular silos would have held considerable grain reserves destined for the preparation of bread. The loaves were baked in molds that accumulated, after discard, on the hills of Dukki Gel (Bonnet 2005, 233–235).

The entrance to the east temple was located on the north side. The doorway, constructed of stone blocks, was in the center of a narrow mudbrick pylon. At the base of a doorpost an inscription in cursive Meroitic was preserved, attributing the temple to Amun. This ancient inscription probably dates to the second century BCE, but the structure itself was certainly built around 500 BCE if we are to believe the rare inscribed blocks. The two

side doors of the courtyard reused the columns of a former New Kingdom building. The next rooms were profoundly disturbed, with an overturned floor partially constructed of talatat, probably recuperated from the central temple. As for the sanctuary with its two chambers, the monumental granite bases must still have been in place to support a naos in front of the transverse chapel to the west and within the sanctuary itself.

Thus the northeast ceremonial palace continued in use for royal ceremonies, to which we must add a new building a bit farther to the north that may have served the same function. The Napatan layers prevent us from uncovering a complete plan: only the rectilinear foundations of cross walls and a circular enclosure have been uncovered. Also worth noting is the presence of a Classic Kerma structure beneath these remains. On an accumulation of sand, the result of climatic shift, a residence was con-

structed in the area near the native religious precinct. Two long rooms, an enclosure, and a work area may have belonged to a farm.

The northeast religious precinct probably underwent the greatest transformation following the destruction by Psammetichus II. A layer of ash and carbonized wood covered the surface once occupied by the two former African-style places of worship (Fig. 82). This destruction prompted the implementation of an unusual architectural program. The main cult building was rebuilt in its original circular form, but only after secreting a remarkable cache. It contained fragments of a wooden naos covered in gold leaf, decorated with a bronze cornice embellished with small plaques of lapis lazuli. This native sanctuary was clearly scorned by the Egyptians, who attempted to obliterate its every trace. It is only after the return of Aspelta that the fragments of this most precious naos were gathered and buried under a silo used for offerings. As he did for the statue fragments, Aspelta wanted to rehabilitate the ancestral kings and this traditional place of worship, probably dedicated to an African god.

The plan of this cult building, so removed from the great classical temples influenced by Egypt, was unique. After a door and an internal porch of sorts, a wide aisle crossed the building to the east (Fig. 83). On the south side of this aisle, small earthen bases created a barrier for a devotional space containing an oval earthen base. On the other side of the aisle, a row of seven supports delimited the sanctuary. Shallowly founded, these columns belonged to low structures of clayey soil probably consolidated with wooden beams. Erected on fire-blackened deposits, the focal point of the cult building was a round pedestal of hardened silt surrounded by the postholes left by a small circular structure. This arrangement is reminiscent of the stone naos that Reisner found at Gebel Barkal, which depicts a circular structure of perishable material, with a Meroitic king accompanied by divine figures on either side of an opening meant for the statue of the god (Wenig 1978, no. 131, 209–210).

Outside the cult building a circle of postholes supported an external roof. In front of the entrance additional curvilinear structures were uncovered, probably associated with monumental entries and an enclosure. Across the entire area as well as in the cult building, we found many crushed jar fragments, along with earth stoppers with seal impressions (Ruffieux 2007, 228–239). The stoppers, numbering in the hundreds, were gathered into large piles both inside the building and outside, in front of the large wooden structures next to the doors. Thus we have evidence for ceremonies, including the pouring of libations, that took place in the religious precinct. The seal impressions are poorly preserved but probably date to the Napatan Period (Bonnet 2009, 98–108).

Returning to the center of the religious complex during the Napatan Period, we note that the vast space between the two Egyptian-style temples was certainly the site of important functions. The institution of the "House of Gold" immediately comes to mind, as illustrated in the decorated quarter of Thutmose III associated with the Temple of Amun at Karnak. Workshops were staffed by

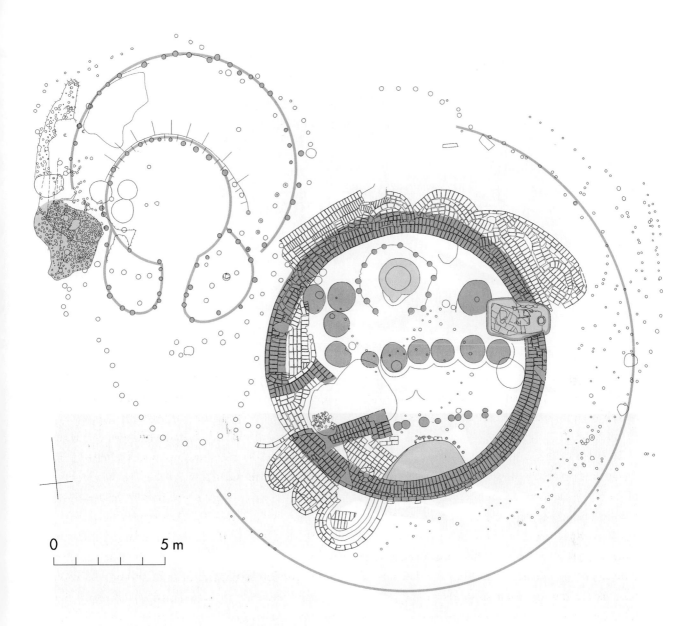

0   5 m

priests and servants. In our case, although the area is not yet completely cleared, we have already found a bronze workshop established in the New Kingdom and transformed during the Twenty-Fifth Dynasty. A solid wall enclosed a quadrilateral area with several furnaces for the melting of bronze objects. North of the porticoed transverse passage, three pits 2.50 to 3 meters deep contained ceramic material from the Classic Kerma Period. The south pit also had a fragmentary stela of Ramesses II, and in the central pit we found

forty pieces belonging to seven monumental stone statues (Fig. 84).

This cache, together with the one in the nearby native temple, yielded statues of great artistic as well as historical interest. They are evidence of the high artistic level that local workshops attained, rivaling the best Egyptian production (Bonnet and Valbelle 2007, 70–139). Aspelta's envoys, charged with recovering the fragments of these statues, also collected the materials that decorated them: hammered gold leaf, gypsum with cloth impressions for fixing

Fig. 84 The cache of royal statues, Dukki Gel

Fig. 85 Partially excavated statue cache

gold leaf, small plaques of lapis lazuli, and pieces of glass. Certain portions of the statues were roughened to facilitate the adhesion of gypsum and cloth, making it possible to reconstruct the exact placement of decorative features.

The statues of Pharaohs Taharqa and Tanutamon and kings Senkamanisken, Anlamani, and Aspelta were reconstructed almost in their entirety; few fragments were missing. We chose to reassemble the sculptures without restoring the missing parts, and despite these gaps, the statues are exceptionally evocative. Their surfaces were finely polished, the work of much higher quality than other statuary from the site. The fragments were arranged in the pit with the head at the bottom, the body parts in the middle, and the bases with feet still attached at the top and to the side. We must acknowledge that, despite the damage it caused, secreting these images of ancestral rulers in a special religious space was a means of perpetuating the cult (Fig. 85).

Great care was taken in dismembering the statues; a master sculptor must have been in charge during the expedition of Psammetichus II. The chisel blows, extremely regular, were carefully placed to break apart the stone. The line of breakage was always at the neck, thus preserving the head intact. *Mekes* cases, symbols of power, were also preserved, as if the sculptor tasked with the destruction respected both the quality of the sculpture and the power of these enemy kings. Traces of pigment are still visible, as in the white and red of the crowns of Upper and Lower Egypt. Especially interesting is that the statue of Anlamani was completely covered in a black wash still adhering to the stone. Originally the statues were richly decorated with ornaments and paint, projecting an image of wealth and grandeur (Fig. 86).

The sculptures of Dukki Gel are comparable to those discovered at Gebel Barkal, where two caches yielded monumental statues of the very same rulers (Bonnet and Valbelle 2007). They were found in annexes close to Temples B500 and B800. Sad to say, only a portion of these sacred deposits remained in situ, several pieces having been pillaged by treasure hunters. After the statues were broken during the military campaign of Psammetichus II, their fragments were arranged in a specific order, most likely at the behest of Aspelta, who wanted the cult of the ancestral kings to resume in these sacred places.

Fig. 86   Statue of King Anlamani

Once again, as at Dukki Gel, a skilled sculptor was in charge of dismembering the statues, and he did so with great respect. Chisel blows aimed at the neck preserved the head intact. The dorsal pillar inscribed with the names of the king and the god Amun of Napata, as well as the torso with its loincloth, were preserved in most cases. The arms were sometimes separated from the body and the lower part of the legs almost systematically broken.

Burnt beams, the result of destruction by Egyptian troops, were also found in the deposit of Temple B800 (Reisner 1917, 1918, 1920), possibly the remnants of a shelter erected to protect the statues. A thick layer of black soil with traces of fire and sculptural fragments may have been laid down after the conflict. Objects in the rubble may be associated with the statues, either decorative elements or offerings deposited at the feet of the statues. Reisner described faience vessels, small statue fragments, pendants, and beads possibly belonging to ornaments attached to the stone. In the Dukki Gel cache, we also found fine statue fragments from the New Kingdom associated with sacred deposits. Aspelta's envoys obviously bore them in mind during their reorganization.

In 2007, statues of the same kings were uncovered in reconstructed levels below the remains of the Meroitic temple at Dangeil. The site is far from the great Napatan metropolises, and several people have questioned whether the Egyptian troops of Psammetichus II actually passed through this area on their way south. However, certain features of these statues are identical to those from the caches of Gebel Barkal and Dukki Gel, and are part of a deposit that received the same treatment (Anderson and Mohamed Ahmed 2014, 613–619). Perhaps the sack of Dangeil occurred during the pursuit of Aspelta and his army, and once Aspelta was able to return, he reestablished order in the liberated city. The few fragments recovered are of three kings only, Taharqa, Senkamanisken, and Aspelta, but the statues were probably first placed in a cache that was later robbed. Fragments of stone bear the characteristic chisel marks noted elsewhere, and we can assume that the same Egyptian sculptor broke apart the royal sculptures of Dangeil during the expedition of Psammetichus II. Once again he left the head intact and separated the body from the legs.

An amulet fragment and a pendant with the faience head of a ram were recovered from the same levels as the statue fragments and may be associated with them. This is reminiscent of the statue of Taharqa from Dukki Gel, which was roughened for the attachment of a necklace and pendants. Faience decorative elements were probably added to the statue, which was not to be left unornamented. This discovery in the context of a temple that predates the Meroitic sanctuary is further evidence that royal statues were of first importance during the reconstruction of a city. By burying them, it was possible to preserve the royal ancestor cult.

Aspelta's reconquest is proof of the power of the first Napatan rulers. Let us add, in this historical context, the discovery of several fragments of a granodiorite stela from the third year of the reign of Aspelta, the fourth ruler of the Napatan Dynasty (Valbelle and Rilly 2012). To the fragments inventoried from the destruction levels of the central temple at Dukki Gel may be joined a large fragment of the same stone recovered by the police and returned to the French Section of the Direction of Antiquities of Sudan (SFDAS) in Khartoum. Once the inscription was recovered, Dominique Valbelle quickly established its relationship to the stela from Sanam called the "Adoption Stela," today in the Louvre. By comparison, it is possible to determine the exact measures taken at Pnubs to restore the smooth functioning of the cult following the expedition of Psammetichus II (Valbelle and Rilly 2012, 5). The royal delegation made the arrangements necessary to continue the cult of Amun. The different manifestations of this god were of paramount importance in Nubian cults, especially since they were closely related to the exercise of royal power.

Once the region was pacified, the city of Pnubs took on the role of ceremonial and royal center, while Gebel Barkal, together with Sanam (Napata), held the higher rank of capital. The period in which claims over Egypt were made in various ways appears to have ended. The royal statues from the caches were represented with the traditional Nubian headdress or the crowns of Upper and Lower Egypt, which must have been an intolerable provocation to Psammetichus II, who decided to put an end to it once and for all. We know less about the following centuries at Dukki Gel, but the temples and their outbuildings were very active, and the abundant ceramic material found in the site or in the neighborhood (Mohamed Ahmed 1992) testifies to the development of the entire region.

Dukki Gel in the Meroitic Period

Starting in 300 BCE, there was a progressive transfer of royal power from Napata to Meroë. We do not know much about Dukki Gel in the first centuries of the Meroitic kingdom. We can cull useful historical facts primarily from ancient sources, and we do have the rich archeological record of the "Island of Meroë," the region of Butana in Central Sudan (Baud 2010, 18–75). Textual evidence from Dukki Gel is rare, and besides cursive Meroitic inscriptions on the gate of the east temple, we lack primary sources (Rilly 2009). There is, however, one important line of evidence that aids chronological study: the presence of several structures that include fired brick. The systematic use of this material provides confirmation that several building projects were undertaken at the beginning of our era. Together with ceramic evidence from the Classical Period and some iconographic data, we can propose the reconstruction of the temples during the co-regency of King Natakamani and Kandake Amanitore (Fig. 87).

A RECONSTRUCTED TEMPLE

Construction was thus resumed in the east temple, and a cursive inscription is evidence that the earlier Napatan temple was maintained until Natakamani instituted his building program (Baud 2010, 213–226). The pylon was shifted to the north and rebuilt on a grander plan with two massive sections. A facing of sorts was added to the front, and monumental decorative fragments were found on the ground along the two moles. Pieces of frescoed coating and a large quantity of stucco fragments were spread over the surface. We were able to identify larger-than-life figures with bodies of red ochre, frieze elements, and prophylactic images. A colossal lion's paw in yellow paint attests to the presence of this animal with the royal couple. The face of the pylon, constructed of fired brick, extended for 25 meters. The entrance probably opened into a dismantled stone doorway that was preceded by the paved dromos,

150.00W
100.00W
50.00W
0.00
50.00N
0.00
50.00S
100.00S
150.00S
200.00S
0
20 m

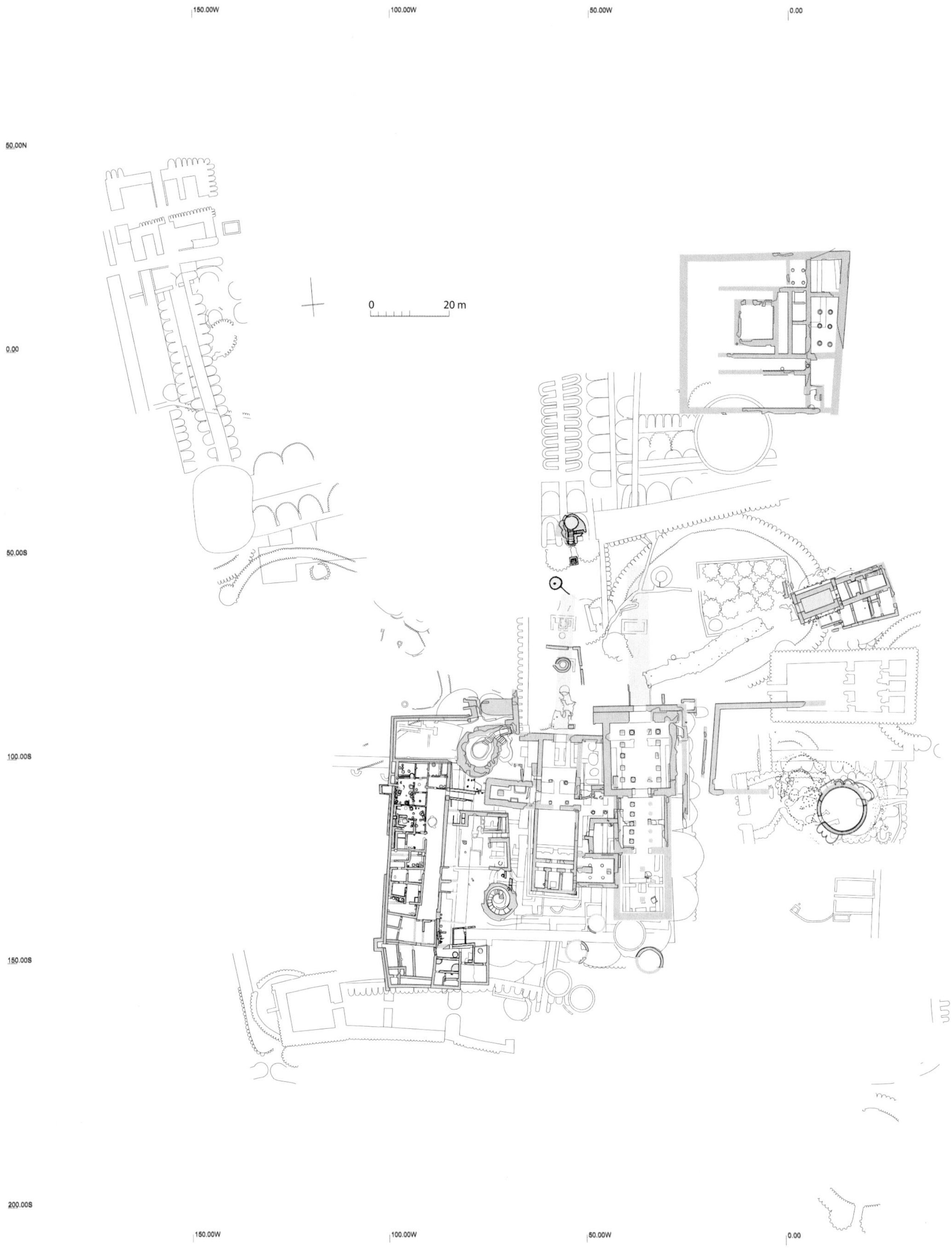

Fig. 87 Schematic plan of Dukki Gel in the Meroitic Period

consolidated on either side by a low wall of sand-stone blocks on a foundation of fired brick and mudbrick. One of the paving stones was engraved with the image of a foot facing outward. This ex-voto image resembles several incised feet both in and in front of the gate of the great temple of Amun at Tabo, dating to the Meroitic Period. The central core of the pylon was constructed of mud-brick, as were the side walls, which were finished with a facing only one fired brick thick. The second doorway of the peristyle courtyard was also consoli-dated with fired brick, extending up to the door-frame and the passage. Walls and a stone pavement can also be reconstructed in this area.

The fourteen column bases in the courtyard were on square foundations that included reused blocks, several of which were decorated with New Kingdom bas-reliefs. Fired-brick masonry was set on top of the foundation stones. The large sandstone column bases, almost completely broken, have been partially reconstructed. Traces of a yellow coating were still distinguishable on some of the fragments. In the southwest corner of the peristyle courtyard, the re-mains of a slightly raised oblong basin with a coated

bottom were preserved. Fired bricks enclosed the basin. After the courtyard was a narrower hypo-style hall with two rows of five columns. The square column foundations were smaller than those of the courtyard and supported narrower columns. The sandstone shafts were also coated in yellow wash. The corner of the west wall establishes the length of the hall at 12 meters long by 11 meters wide (Rondot and Török 2010, 227–233).

The next two rooms, as well as the sanctuary, were dismantled; the tumbled fired-brick fill is evident in the destruction levels. Thus it is possible to propose a length of at least 55 meters for the temple, which would have been one of the largest monuments of the Meroitic Period. The west side chapel was once again assigned to the cult, since its side walls were restored with fired brick and the altar extended up to the wall connected with the wall of the neigh-boring sanctuary. The granite base of the naos, which faced the entrance, was probably preserved in place. This was also the case for the base of the sanctuary that remained in use; the meager remnants of a side wall indicate that a temenos must have enclosed the temple on two sides. Also of note, at

Fig. 88   West side chapel in the Meroitic Period

the northeast corner of the pylon is a small service area constructed of fired brick as well as part of an enclosure that probably protected the dromos.

THE CENTRAL TEMPLE

The dromos of the central temple, consisting of two closely spaced lanes, almost parallel, was one of the important roads leading to the religious precinct. While the Napatan well was preserved, the Kushite fire altar appears to have been abandoned. The alley that separated these features from the temple entrance was probably lined with statues of rams, as two rectangular bases are still identified by several stones in front of the pylon. Most surprising was the excavation of a new well in line with the ceremonial way, approximately 50 meters to the north. This was an impressive well, more than 4 meters in diameter inside a thick wall lined with both fired brick and mudbrick. An axial staircase of reused stone was constructed on an older foundation. Another perpendicular staircase joined the central ramp. Massive mudbrick structures surrounded the access to the well, and a square base to the south must

have anchored a support. Next to the dromos we found a circular enclosure for a tree; the location of the trunk was still visible in the center. A ceramic channel probably protected this low rounded wall of brick of a form familiar in the Meroitic Period. This enclosure may have housed a jujube tree, sacred to the city.

The general plan of the central temple maintained proportions comparable to those of earlier periods. The narrow pylon was constructed of stone above the foundation to provide support for the doorposts. Fired bricks were added to the older mudbrick core, aligned with the side walls. Nothing remains of possible supports north of the courtyard, but the column bases do seem to be preserved in front of the chapel on the west side (Figs. 88 and 89). This chapel, destroyed by fire, was reconstructed on the same plan: that is to say, a narrow sanctuary opening onto a wider space. The altar, practically a cube, consisted of sandstone blocks on an irregular pavement. Rectangular silos were located in front of the chapel from its initial construction; they were enlarged in stages and left only a narrow passage along the length of the building. A large monolithic

threshold of Tumbus granite was part of a complete redesign of the door opening into the courtyard.

On the other side, in the porticoed transverse passage, modifications were carried out in the north colonnade. They included the installation of a ceramic channel and a bread oven. The wide expanse of the hypostyle hall was completely dug up at the end of the Meroitic Period, making it impossible to reconstruct its plan. As for the tripartite sanctuary, it was probably maintained, but the complex is very degraded. The bronze workshop connected to the temples remained in use. Apparently the large ceramic furnaces were of mixed use, since numerous bread molds for the preparation of offerings were found alongside pieces of slag and a rectilinear tuyere. In two of the furnaces, a round duct encircled the central part of the blackened and reddened bottom.

Fig. 89   West side chapel in the Meroitic Period

The trace of the duct was visible in the burnt silt. A crucible fragment contained traces of copper.

A number of small bronze objects were found in this area; they are to be associated with the workshop. Several statuettes of Osiris appear to have been made in one or two of the workshop molds. Other figures and pins with decorated stems were also recovered. As we have seen, bronze manufacture began in this location during the New Kingdom. The walls of the workshop were quite thick, isolating the furnaces from the hypostyle halls on either side. Traffic was directed from the porticoed transverse passage through a long courtyard leading to a central door that was often modified. Stelae fragments were found in the courtyard, along with abundant ceramic material. The area outside the temples to the south was reserved for large circular silos that were used, for some considerable time, for grain storage.

These grain reserves must have been connected to the temple outbuildings that were under constant reconstruction; the number of ovens increased and production units were modified by changing the layout of rooms and courtyards. The outer west-east wall was enlarged and two quadrangular watch-towers added to the enclosure. The long courtyard serving the outbuildings also led to the south residence, where an observation point was maintained to supervise the preparation of temple offerings. The large central building was extended in the direction of the south well. It consisted of three building units and a central courtyard and housed administrative functions connected to the various workshops. The considerable activity in the Napatan and Meroitic outbuildings is evident from the mounds of broken bread molds, ash, and charcoal, quite characteristic of many sites in Sudan. Along with cattle bones, we have proof that offering rites were carried out for millennia, although in the final centuries of the practice the quantity of offerings seems to have increased.

The south well is probably one of the most accomplished constructions of Meroitic architecture. While taking into account the spiral staircase constructed in the early New Kingdom, the master builder constructed a well 6 meters in diameter on the inside and 8 meters on the outside with an internal staircase. The masonry of the well wall, in fired brick, alternated in attractive courses of flat bricks with bricks set on edge. At a depth of 6 or 7 meters, the staircase met the stone circle of a New Kingdom well. The masterful technique and aesthetic quality of the interior staircase, constructed of reused structural blocks, are proof enough that the two constructions complemented each other. Indeed, five additional steps were sunk into the earlier well, and against the first step a block decorated with a royal foot was still in situ. The foot symbolically crushes two Nubian prisoners on either side whose arms are bound by the *sema* hieroglyph (a symbol for the union of Upper and Lower Egypt). This fine relief also depicts a typical Kushite headdress.

The north well, 18 meters in diameter, is more eroded. During the Meroitic Period the edge was terraced, cutting little by little into the *galous* structure. A staircase of reused stone was added to the northeast, tangential in relation to the well. The original oblong masonry was later cut into and perhaps replaced by a new perpendicular stair dug into the alluvial silt. The steps were consolidated with fired brick and mudbrick. The outbuildings also must have had access to the well through a corridor that ended with a door and

stone reinforcements above the well. On the north side, a robust terrace was constructed in place of the previous ceremonial arrangement, with a narrow passage leading to a small platform over the well. In this passage we found a remarkable bronze processional incense burner that was probably mounted on a staff.

The religious precinct included a vast rectangular walled area on the side of the circular place of worship. An earlier low wall probably belonged to an original installation in this area. It is possible that an earlier building project was undertaken here, since structural blocks were abandoned in large quantities and not used. The enclosure wall, aligned with the face of the east temple pylon, appears to postdate the temple. This wall was also aligned with the south wall of the peristyle courtyard and may have been part of a contemporary building phase that resulted in the elimination of the outbuildings of the native sanctuary. The function of this ceremonial area remains unclear, as its remains were very close to the surface. Circular pits, random in nature, were dug into the ground. They may have been part of a garden or grove of trees, but these remains, too, were quite poorly preserved. We must also take into account the actions of *sebbakhin,* farmers in search of a fertilizer often found along the riverbank.

TWO PALACES

The mudbrick rooms in the New Kingdom ceremonial palace were transformed several times during this period. However, the door that may have been where the king made his appearances seems to have been maintained with little change, due perhaps to the great care taken in its construction. The addition of fired bricks around the walls of the building indicates a desire to preserve this ancient palace during the reign of Natakamani. This restoration of the palace is especially remarkable when we consider the many centuries it was in use. Its preservation is particularly puzzling because an enormous palace was constructed immediately to the north and must already have existed during Napatan times. Once again we have evidence for continuous occupation in this area, due in part to the respect accorded to

an ancient palace that was considered sanctified in some way.

The north palace was rebuilt in a style well known in the Meroitic Empire: for example, the famous monument B1500 at Gebel Barkal, and the palaces of Wad Ben Naga, Muweis, and Meroë 7507 (Maillot 2015, 27–34; 2014, 783–795). These buildings were square in plan, measuring more than 60 meters to a side, with an upper floor. They were arranged around a central space with typical doors in the center of each side; sometimes side entrances led down to numerous basement storerooms. We could add to this list quite a few more similar structures of more modest proportions, including the palace at Dukki Gel, which measured 40 meters to a side. A light well illuminated both floors of the building. Despite the mediocre state of preservation, we were able to observe the remnants of Nubian vaults collapsed into oblong rooms. Two rooms with four and six columns, respectively, were preserved to the east, where the remains of an earlier building required the master builder to leave in place a substantial wall at an angle to support the east façade.

Conclusion

The archaeological discoveries presented here have added considerably to our historical understanding of this part of Africa, opening a new field of research into the evolution of the local kingdoms that steadfastly resisted Egyptian domination. These developments must, however, be examined in the context of the trade networks upon which Egypt depended, which led to repeated conflicts as Egypt sought to control the exchange of goods. Given the extent of our knowledge about the land of the Pharaohs, it was long since past time for us to focus on the roots of the Nubian and Central Sudanese populations. We are convinced that the historical origins of the African continent are to be found in these regions, and that many native populations maintained their individuality despite the currents of influence from the Mediterranean Basin and the Near East that reached Central Africa through Egypt. Further study is needed to prove this hypothesis, but already we are able to report that African traditions were marked by a strong originality that remains to be fully understood (Fig. 90).

It is perhaps the fortifications that reveal most strikingly the differences between the Central Af-

rican approach and the Egyptian reaction, especially in the manner in which highly trained armies resisted advancing troops. Starting in the Old Kingdom, fortresses were established in Nubia and soon formed a fortified line at the Second Cataract that barred passage in a geographically hostile region known as Batn el-Hajar, the "Belly of Rocks." Fearing the worst, the mighty empire strove to defend itself with an impregnable line as early as 2000 BCE. Our own discoveries have brought to light the vestiges of singular defensive systems, evidence of a complex military architecture quite distant from other examples to which it may be compared.

Equally unique was the urban layout of a city protected by two fortified enclosures whose gates are distinguished by their astonishing proportions. They were constructed between double towers, often preceded by immense hypostyle halls. These halls, either oval or circular in plan, undoubtedly served as locations for the initial exchange of goods and the showcasing of precious items. Judging by later developments, we can perceive a desire to place cult installations directly in these thoroughfares, either in front of the gate or in its immediate vicinity. No-

Fig. 90   The site museum at Kerma

table examples include sacred trees that certainly played an important role at Dukki Gel, where the jujube was frequently mentioned. In any case, these monumental entryways featured a ceremonial architecture specifically designed to impress the visitor.

This architecture, whose techniques we do not yet fully understand, displayed characteristic features that remain to be studied in detail. The use of great quantities of mudbrick was adopted following contact with Egyptians who, since the Old Kingdom, used stone, *galous,* and brick in Nubia (Emery 1963, 116–120). The bricks, which provide a means of studying the phases of construction, were adapted to circular buildings; they demonstrate the mastery of the masons, who certainly were recruited from the local population. The immense circular foundations were constructed of perfectly laid masonry. We note that bricks were frequently perforated by posts built into the walls, a simple way to consolidate façades that often had connected bastions as well. Although we have not found them, we can nevertheless reconstruct the presence of horizontal wooden beams placed at regular intervals and forming a skeleton that ensured the stability of the structure.

Fig. 91 Early Kerma ceramic bowl

We must remember that the earliest occupation levels remain unknown. From the beginning of our investigations at Dukki Gel, we followed horizontal layers and avoided excavating to any significant depth (Fig. 91). It is quite clear that the African city predated Classic Kerma; the many overlaps already described are evidence of a long period of development. Elsewhere, we know that the city extended well beyond the actual limits of the protected site, and our reconstructions take this fact into account. Our picture of this ceremonial city will not be complete without residential quarters, which doubtless included a great number of circular structures as well as base camps to quarter troops in times of conflict (Fig. 92).

In our current state of knowledge, one of the defining characteristics of the African city is the considerable number of places of worship. Equally noteworthy is the proliferation of offering tables, not only along ceremonial pathways and at the intersections of passages but also in special installations in the palaces and a chapel. As for the cult buildings themselves, they were often surrounded by well-constructed buttresses and distinctive rounded bastions. Fortified entrances (Fig. 93) led to long corridors. Inside the cult area, the practice was to install a central pedestal or a privileged area separated by stakes. The superstructure that protected this sacred area was probably vaulted. Taking into account the lack of space, we can reconstruct, on the pedestals preceded by two or three steps, a wooden naos for the statue of the god.

The *mnnw* of Thutmose I radically changed the plan of the city as this institution was bound by different rules that the Egyptian architects were obliged to respect. Pharaonic models predominated, but still the general layout appeared to take into account the functions of earlier buildings. It may have differed in form, but an imposing religious center continued in use, probably accompanied by more modest buildings. The ceremonial palaces were replaced by two large oblong buildings with well-proportioned hypostyle halls. Numerous silos held food reserves. As for the fortifications, they reverted to a Nubian system of connected bastions; the two enclosures were removed. At the same time, however, new defensive fronts were evidence of overwhelming power. The dromos providing central access to the main

Fig. 92   Middle Kerma bronze objects

Fig. 93   Terra-cotta seal carved with
the representation of a gate, Classic
Kerma

temple with its hypostyle hall played an important role in the ceremonial life of the city.

The Egyptian architect's response to the African style of construction was to replace entry vestibules with foregates and inner gates of truly extravagant proportions. The construction of great structures projecting from the city walls, which obliterated the earlier circular or oval entry halls, was a demonstration of the military power of the new administration and clearly designed to impress the local population. But as impregnable as these constructions were, they also had a ceremonial function, if we are to believe the multiplication of columns in relation to the alleyways. We must also consider the altar in the northern extension that continued to be maintained during the restorations by Hatshepsut. And finally, the existence of several hypostyle halls and seats, installed to monitor traffic, is evidence of a system conceived specifically to supervise merchandise entering the complex. In the foregate at Mirgissa, Brigitte Gratien inventoried great quantities of seal impressions, additional proof that these gates housed administrative functions (Gratien, personal communication).

The reconquest by a Nubian and African coalition represented an exceptional historical phase. It is rare to be able to verify textual evidence with the archaeological record, and we are fortunate indeed to have material remains from this transitional period. It is quite clear that the major preoccupation of the native population was defense, which was organized along very different lines than the Egyptian model. The temples were surrounded by enclosures with connected bastions. In the northeast quarter, fortifications were continually strengthened and repaired. As for the central precinct, it too was surrounded by bastioned walls, thus forming an isolated unit; traces of fire observed to the north provide ample evidence that hostile actions took place there.

Modifications carried out by the coalition are harder to define in the area of the northeast gate, apart from the enormous towers located at the northern end. The gate itself, with its closing device, was reoriented in line with the side alleyway of Thutmose I. In front of this monumental entry, several circular areas consolidated by small buttresses protected ritual platforms probably designed for the deposit of offerings. One of these platforms was roofed by a light rectangular superstructure, reconstructed from its six column bases. Other similar circles have not yet been excavated, but the ensemble as a whole is evidence of an enigmatic ritual, doubtless religious in nature. Numerous tower foundations farther to the north formed a line of defense that appears to be contemporary with the ritual installation. The reconquest, which lasted only a few years, nevertheless left behind impressive structures.

The second *mnnw* returned to the layout of Pnubs, the city of Dukki Gel. Here, too, was a rare opportunity for the archaeologist: to determine how Thutmose II and Hatshepsut modified the plans while preserving the architectural intent of their father, Thutmose I. The enclosure was reestablished in its entirety and strengthened with connected bastions. The north gate was preserved as it was, while the number of columns was doubled in the hypostyle hall leading to the main temple. The columns, some of which were preserved up to a meter in height, must have been taller. They served to remind the local population of the former palaces, now destroyed. One of the palaces was abandoned; the

other was extended and provided with a more imposing façade. Stone blocks were used in the restoration of the temple entrances in the religious center as well as in the hypostyle halls. This major change in building material required a change in methods of construction; thus the arrival of Egyptian artisans. While building methods may have changed, however, the plans of the former cult buildings, now entirely leveled, were preserved. It is remarkable with what fidelity the Egyptian builders reproduced the former temples, while at the same time increasing their grandeur. The sanctuaries themselves were maintained in their original mudbrick state, and we must ask ourselves if the coalition left these places of worship untouched (Fig. 94). Perhaps some respect for the gods of Egypt was observed during the destructions. In the northeast quarter the principal place of worship was enlarged and a fortified corridor added to the entrance; the African gods were thus honored and the scale of the building increased.

The northwest gate and its foregate were restored along colossal proportions, measuring more than 100 meters in length. On the south end, two

Fig. 94   Ram protome from the temple of Hatshepsut

massive oval structures exceeding 30 meters in diameter defined the gate itself. These structures completely overwhelmed the former plan. A series of double wooden posts consolidated the foundations and provided a firm footing. While the foregate returned to the general plan of Thutmose I, the north end was greatly enlarged with a monumental front with several hypostyle halls and a transverse columned portico, probably for use by a rather intrusive administration. The long access roads were also provided with columns, thus emphasizing the ceremonial aspect of the complex. We do not yet know where this special axis led; it ends against a fairly high hill. Excavations planned for our next season may reveal an African place of worship at this location.

When the death of Hatshepsut freed Thutmose III from the constraints of the regency, the power of the Pharaoh once again put its stamp upon the ancient city of Pnubs. With the countryside pacified, the construction of fortifications was unnecessary, and a much simpler enclosure extending over a wide area to the north changed the general plan of the city. Our excavations make it clear that the religious center of Pnubs, where two temples were preserved, remained the focal point of the urban area as a whole. The abandonment of the city of Kerma brought about the regrouping of the population at Dukki Gel, which became a true Nubian metropolis. From that moment on, and continuing throughout the New Kingdom, we can follow the evolution of this site, colonized by Egypt. Our understanding of

Fig. 95   Reconstructed statues in the Kerma Museum: the heart of the collection

Egyptian history is particularly complete for the Eighteenth Dynasty; after that, the influence of the north progressively diminished. At the same time a rising regional metropolis was developing by stages at Gebel Barkal, 200 kilometers to the south, and preparing for the birth of an independent country.

The authorities of this country in the making favored Egyptianization as a means of establishing power on the model of Egypt. As we can see by the burial customs, the local population resisted change and continued to bury their dead in a contracted position, accompanied by grave goods. The elite and their families, however, were interred in painted sarcophagi placed in funerary chambers surmounted by a pyramid. Around 700 BCE, the Twenty-Fifth Dynasty marked a turning point, when Nubian kings took control of the destiny of Egypt and became the rulers of the two countries. The city of Pnubs regained a cer-

tain splendor and many of its monuments were reconstructed. The expedition of Psammetichus II and the destruction of the city also provide the archaeologist with important historical information.

The discovery of a cache with seven monumental statues of Nubian rulers, broken apart into forty pieces, evokes the violence of the conflict (Fig. 95). The circular sanctuary in the northeast part of Dukki Gel was set on fire and destroyed. Nubian military may have threatened the Egyptian Pharaohs; the intervention of Psammetichus II may have prevented new assaults. Besides, the Nubian troops under the command of Aspelta may have maintained their strength once they retreated to Meroë, probably for strategic reasons, where Aspelta had established relations. His return to Dukki Gel is well attested by a substantial building program for the administration; construction increased greatly

Fig. 96   Royal statues in the Kerma Museum

under Aspelta and urban development continued uninterrupted. Substantial residences have been uncovered to the west beneath houses of the modern city. They provide evidence of the wealth of the inhabitants and the settlement of territory distant from Dukki Gel. Urbanization was taking place across a much wider area, well outside the perimeter of the earlier city.

In the Meroitic Period, the city expanded and several cult buildings and a palace were erected. The rapid demographic expansion that took place during this long period is visible in the vast necropolises that covered the ruins of the ancient city of Kerma and its port quarter, as well as the area around Dukki Gel itself. The regular preparation of temple offerings was a major activity, as evidenced by the extensive bakery complex and substantial mounds of bread molds around the central quarter. The construction of a new palace north of the temples was accompanied by the rebuilding, in fired brick, of the old ceremonial palace of the New Kingdom. Other urban spaces certainly existed: we found a New Kingdom building, also restored with fired brick, 400 meters farther north. Geomagnetic surveys have revealed

large Meroitic buildings and an enclosure wall on the south part of the site.

Our archaeological explorations at Dukki Gel have brought to light buildings belonging to little-known periods in Nubia. Further work is necessary fully to interpret these remains, whose levels are easily confused with other well-dated phases. The identification of this African city is a vital contribution to the history of the continent, although only the verified and stratified data that will come from many forthcoming years of study will confirm these preliminary results. Another concern is the archaeological deposits under cultivated fields, which increase the area under study tenfold. What is absolutely essential, as a result of our discoveries, is to complete our understanding of Central Sudan. Kingdoms in this region probably held sway over vast territories; this is, after all, the heart of Africa, and we know very little about it as yet. As a first step, the identification of urban areas and development of a chronology will provide vital comparative data. Already the Italian excavations at Kassala have established a relationship with the Kingdom of Kerma; identical material is found at both sites

dating back to the Old Kingdom. The cultures of the third to first millennia BCE were instrumental in the birth of a true African identity, of which we have caught only a glimpse during the last few centuries. The understanding gained during fifty years of research at Kerma and Dukki Gel allows us to assess the wealth of the African continent—and also to emphasize the need for an extensive research program. The trade routes are very ancient, and human activity has demonstrated its role as a bearer of culture. Egypt benefited from these exchanges and provoked, albeit indirectly, the rise of Nubia, which played an important role as an intermediate state between the Egyptian and Mediterranean worlds, on the one hand, and between Egypt and Central Africa, on the other. Although we may lack a full understanding of the originality of this African world, it still has the power to fascinate, even if we know much more about its recent history than we do about its formative phases (Fig. 96).

Chronology

The following periods are covered in the text.

Periods

Paleolithic	1,000,000–9000 BCE
Mesolithic	9000–6600 BCE
Neolithic	6000–3500 BCE
Pre-Kerma	3500–2500 BCE
Early Kerma	2500–2050 BCE
Middle Kerma	2050–1750 BCE
Classic Kerma	1750–1500 BCE
New Kingdom: Eighteenth to Twentieth Dynasties	1500–1080 BCE
Kushite Kingdoms: Twenty-Fifth Dynasty	750–650 BCE
Napata	650–400 BCE
Meroë	400 BCE–400 CE

Bibliography

Anderson, J. R., and Salah Mohamed Ahmed. 2014. "The Early Kushite Royal Statues at Dangeil, Sudan." In *The Fourth Cataract and Beyond: Proceedings of the 12th International Conference for Nubian Studies,* edited by J. Anderson and D. Welsby, 613–619. Leuven.

Arkell, A. J. 1951–1952. "The History of Darfur, A.D. 1200–1700." *Sudan Notes and Records* 32:207–238 and 33:244–275.

Arkell, A. J. 1961. *A History of the Sudan: From the Earliest Times to 1821.* 2nd ed. London.

Badawy, A. 1968. *A History of Egyptian Architecture: The Empire (the New Kingdom).* Berkeley.

Baud, M. 2010. "Méroé, un monde urbain." In *Méroé, un empire sur le Nil,* edited by M. Baud, 213–226. Paris.

Bietak, M. 1968. *Studien zur Chronologie der Nubischen C-Gruppe. Ein Beitrag zur Frühgeschichte Unternubiens zwischen 2200 und 1550 vor Chr.* Denkschrift der Österreichischen Akademie der Wissenschaften in Wien 97. Vienna.

Bonnet, C. 1978. "Fouilles archéologiques à Kerma (Soudan). Rapport préliminaire de la campagne 1977–1978." *Genava,* n.s., 26:107–134.

Bonnet, C. 1980. "Les fouilles archéologiques de Kerma (Soudan)." *Genava,* n.s., 28:31–62.

Bonnet, C. 1985. "Aperçu sur l'architecture civile de Kerma." *Cahier de Recherches de l'Institut de Papyrologie et d'Égyptologie de Lille* 7:11–21.

Bonnet, C. 1986. "Un atelier de bronziers à Kerma." In *Nubische Studien. Tagungsakten der 5. internationalen Konferenz der International Society for Nubian Studies: Heidelberg, 22.–25. September 1982,* 19–22. Mainz.

Bonnet, C. 1995. "Les fouilles archéologiques de Kerma (Soudan)." *Genava,* n.s., 43:31–52.

Bonnet, C. 1999a. "Les fouilles archéologiques de Kerma (Soudan)." *Genava,* n.s., 47:57–76.

Bonnet, C. 1999b. "The Funerary Traditions of Middle Nubia." In *Recent Research in Kushite History and Archaeology, Proceedings of the 8th International Conference for Meroitic Studies,* edited by D. Welsby, 251–256. British Museum Occasional Paper 131. London.

Bonnet, C. 2001. "Kerma. Rapport préliminaire sur les campagnes de 1999–2000 et 2000–2001." *Genava,* n.s., 49:197–218.

Bonnet, C. 2003. "Kerma. Rapport préliminaire sur les campagnes de 2001–2002 et 2002–2003." *Genava,* n.s., 51:257–280.

Bonnet, C. 2005. "Le site de Doukki Gel, l'enceinte de la ville égyptienne et les travaux de restauration." *Genava,* n.s., 53:227–238.

Bonnet, C. 2007. "La ville de Doukki Gel après les derniers chantiers archéologiques." *Genava,* n.s., 55:187–200.

Bonnet, C. 2009. "Un ensemble religieux nubien devant une forteresse égyptienne du début de la XVIIIe dynastie." *Genava,* n.s., 57:95–108.

Bonnet, C. 2011a. "Le site archéologique de Tabo: une nouvelle réflexion." In *La pioche et la plume. Autour du Soudan, du Liban et de la Jordanie. Hommages archéologiques à Patrice Lenoble,* edited by J.-M. Ela, 283–293. Paris.

Bonnet, C. 2011b. "Les deux villes égyptienne et nubienne de Doukki Gel." *Genava,* n.s., 59:7–16.

Bonnet, C. 2012. "Les grands monuments égyptiens et nubiens du début de la XVIIIe dynastie sur le site de Doukki Gel (Kerma)." *Bulletin de l'Institut Français d'Archéologie Orientale* 112:57–75.

Bonnet, C. 2013. "Découverte d'une nouvelle ville cérémonielle nubienne et le *menenou* de Thoutmosis Ier (Doukki Gel, Soudan)." *Comptes Rendus de l'Académie des Inscriptions et Belles-Lettres* 2 (April–June): 807–823.

Bonnet, C. 2015a. "Les royaumes de Kouch et de Napata." *Egypte, Afrique et Orient* 78 (June–August): 19–26.

Bonnet, C. 2015b. "Une ville cérémonielle africaine du début du Nouvel Empire égyptien." *Bulletin de l'Institut Français d'Archéologie Orientale* 115:1–14.

Bonnet, C. 2017. "From the Nubian Temples and Palaces of Dokki Gel to an Egyptian *Mnnw* during the Beginning of Dynasty 18." In *Nubia in the New Kingdom: Lived Experience, Pharaonic Control and Indigenous Traditions. British Museum Publications on Egypt and Sudan 3,* edited by N. Spencer, A. Stevens, and M. Binder, 107–122. Leuven.

Bonnet, C., and M. Honegger. 2005a. "Les fouilles archéologiques de Kerma (Soudan). Rapport préliminaire sur les campagnes de 2003–2004 et 2004–2005." *Genava,* n.s., 53:223–226.

Bonnet, C., and D. Valbelle. 1980. "Un prêtre d'Amon de Pnoubs enterré à Kerma." *Bulletin de l'Institut Français d'Archéologie Orientale* 80: 3–12.

Bonnet, C., and D. Valbelle. 2000. *Edifices et rites funéraires à Kerma.* Paris.

Bonnet, C., and D. Valbelle. 2004. *Le temple principal de la ville de Kerma et son quartier religieux.* Paris.

Bonnet, C., and D. Valbelle. 2007. *The Nubian Pharaohs: Black Kings on the Nile.* Cairo.

Bonnet, C., and D. Valbelle. 2014. *La ville de Kerma, une capitale nubienne au sud de l'Egypte.* Lausanne.

Bourriau, J. 2004. "Egyptian Pottery Found in Kerma Ancien, Kerma Moyen and Kerma Classique Graves at Kerma." In *Nubian Studies 1998: Proceedings of the Ninth Conference of the International Society of Nubian Studies, August 21–26, 1998, Boston, Massachusetts,* edited by T. Kendall, 3–13. Boston.

Denyer, S. 1978. *African Traditional Architecture.* London.

Emery, W. B. 1963. "Egypt Exploration Society, Preliminary Report on the Excavations at Buhen, 1962." *Kush* 11:116–120.

Emery, W. B., H. S. Smith, and A. Millard. 1979. *The Fortress of Buhen: The Archaeological Report.* London.

Gabolde, L. 2004. "La stèle de Thoutmosis II à Assouan, témoin historique et archétype littéraire." *Orientalia Monspeliensa* 14:129–148.

Gratien, B. 1978. *Les cultures Kerma. Essai de classification.* Lille.

Gratien, B. 1990. "Les Egyptiens en Nubie, politique et administration aux 3e et 2e millénaires avant J.-C." Doctoral thesis, Université de la Sorbonne, Paris IV.

Gratien, B. 1991. "Empreintes de sceaux et administration à Kerma (Kerma Classique)." *Genava,* n.s., 39:21–24.

Gratien, B. 1993. "Nouvelles empreintes de sceaux à Kerma, aperçus sur l'administration de Kouch au milieu du deuxième millénaire avant J.-C." *Genava,* n.s., 41:27–32.

Gratien, B. (dir.), R.-P. Dissaux, J. Evrard, S. Marchi, G. Nogara, and D. Usai. 2013. *Abou Sofyan et Zankor, Prospections dans le Kordofan occidental (Soudan).* Lille.

Griffith, F. L. 1923. "Oxford Excavations in Nubia: The Cemetery of Sanam." *Liverpool Annals* 10:73–171.

Jacquet-Gordon, H. 1981. "A Tentative Typology of Egyptian Bread Moulds." In *Studien zur altägyptischen Keramik,* edited by D. Arnold, 11–24. Mainz.

Kemp, B. J. 1989. *Ancient Egypt: Anatomy of a Civilization.* London.

Kemp, B. J. 2012. *The City of Akhenaton and Nefertiti: Amarna and Its People.* London.

Kendall, T. 2009. "Talatat Architecture at Jebel Barkal." *Sudan and Nubia* 13:2–16.

Kendall, T. 2014. "Reused Relief Blocks of Piankhy from B900 toward a Decipherment of the Osiris Cult at Jebel Barkal." In *The Fourth Cataract and Beyond: Proceedings of the 12th International Conference for Nubian Studies,* edited by J. Anderson and D. Welsby, 663–686. Leuven.

Laboury, D. 2010. *Akhénaton, les grands pharaons.* Paris.

Lepsius, K. R. 1913. *Denkmäler aus Aegypten und Aethiopen, Text, herausgegeben von Eduard Naville.* Vol. V. Leipzig.

Maillot, M. 2014. "The Palace of Muweis in the Shendi Reach: A Comparative Approach." In *The Fourth Cataract and Beyond: Proceedings of the 12th International Conference for Nubian Studies,* edited by J. Anderson and D. Welsby, 783–795. Leuven.

Maillot, M. 2015. "Architecture et urbanisme du royaume de Méroé," *Égypte, Afrique et Orient* 78:27–34.

Manzo, A. 2012. "From the Sea to the Desert and Back: New Research in Eastern Sudan." *British Museum Studies in Ancient Egypt and Sudan* 18:75–106.

Marchi, S. 2017. "Entre arrière-pays et capitale, l'approvisionnement et le stockage des céréales dans le royaume de Kerma (Soudan)." *NeHeT* 5:197–216.

Marchi, S. forthcoming. "Water for Temples and Palaces: The Wells of Dokki Gel during the Napatan and Meroitic Periods." *Proceedings of the 12th International Conference for Meroitic Studies.*

Masquelier-Loorius, J. 2013. *Séthi Ier et le début de la XIXe dynastie.* Paris.

Mohamed Ahmed, Salah El-Din. 1992. *L'agglomération napatéenne de Kerma. Enquête archéologique et ethnographique en milieu urbain.* Paris.

Monnier, F. 2010. *Les forteresses égyptiennes du prédynastique au Nouvel Empire.* Connaissance de l'Egypte ancienne 22. Brussels.

Moriset, S., L. M. Dixey, J. Muwanga Sembuya, T. Joffroy, E. Kamuhangire, and R. Kigongo. 2011. *Kasubi Tombs, Uganda-Kampala.* 2nd ed. Pout de Claix.

Morkot, R. 2000. *The Black Pharaohs: Egypt's Nubian Rulers.* London

Privati, B. 1999. "La céramique de la nécropole orientale de Kerma (Soudan): essai de classification." *Cahier de Recherches de l'Institut de Papyrologie et d'Égyptologie de Lille* 20:41–69.

Privati, B. 2004. "Kerma: classification des céramiques de la nécropole orientale." *Nubian Studies 1998: Proceedings of the Ninth Conference of the International Society of Nubian Studies. August 21–26, 1998, Boston, Massachusetts,* edited by T. Kendall, 145–156. Boston.

Push, E. P. 1991. "Recent Work at Northern Piramesse: Results of Excavations by the Pelizaeus-Museum, Hildesheim at Qantir." In *Fragments of a Shattered Visage: The Proceedings of the International Symposium on Ramesses the Great,* edited by E. Bleiberg and R. Freed, 201–202. Monographs of the Institute of Egyptian Art and Archeology. Memphis, TN.

Reisner, G. A. 1917, 1918, 1920. "The Barkal Temples in 1916." *Journal of Egyptian Archaeology* 4:213–227; 5:99–112; 6:247–264.

Reisner, G. A. 1923a. *Excavations at Kerma, Parts I–III.* Harvard African Studies 5. Cambridge, MA.

Reisner, G. A. 1923b. *Excavations at Kerma, Parts IV–V.* Harvard African Studies 6. Cambridge, MA.

Rilly, C. 2009. *Le Méroïtique et sa famille linguistique.* Louvain.

Roccati, A. 1982. *La littérature historique sous l'Ancien Empire égyptien.* Paris.

Rondot, V., and Török, L. 2010. "La Maison du Dieu: le Temple." In *Méroé, un empire sur le Nil,* edited by M. Baud, 227–233. Paris.

Ruffieux, P. 2005. "La céramique de Doukki Gel découverte au cours des campagnes 2003–2004 et 2004–2005." *Genava,* n.s., 53:255–263.

Ruffieux, P. 2007. "Ensembles céramiques napatéens découverts durant les campagnes 2005–2006 et 2006–2007 à Doukki Gel (Kerma)." *Genava,* n.s., 60:223–239.

Ruffieux, P. 2009. "Poteries découvertes dans un temple égyptien de la XVIIIe dynastie à Doukki Gel (Kerma)." *Genava,* n.s., 57:121–134.

Smith, H. S. 1966. "Kor: Report of the Excavations of the Egypt Exploration Society at Kor, 1965." *Kush* 14: 187–243.

Smith, H. S., W. B. Emery, B. J. Kemp, G. T. Martin, and D. B. O'Connor. 1976. *The Fortress of Buhen: The Inscriptions.* London.

Somaglino, C. 2010. "Etude lexicographique du terme *mnnw.*" Université de Paris IV.

Trigger, B. 1976. *Nubia under the Pharaohs.* London.

Valbelle, D. 1999. "Kerma: les inscriptions." *Genava,* n.s., 47:83–86.

Valbelle, D. 2001. "Kerma: les inscriptions." *Genava,* n.s., 49:229–234.

Valbelle, D. 2003. "Kerma: les inscriptions et la statuaire." *Genava,* n.s., 51:291–300.

Valbelle, D. 2005a. "Hatchepsout en Nubie." *Bulletin de la Société Française d'Égyptologie* 167:33–50.

Valbelle, D. 2005b. "Kerma. Les inscriptions et la statuaire." *Genava,* n.s., 53:251–254.

Valbelle, D. 2008. "Les temples thoutmosides de Pnoubs (Doukki Gel). L'apport de l'épigraphie et de l'iconographie." In *Between the Cataracts: Proceedings of the 11th Conference for Nubian Studies, Warsaw University, 2006*, 85–93. Warsaw.

Valbelle, D. 2013. "Comment les Egyptiens du début de la XVIIIe dynastie désignaient les Kouchites et leurs alliés." *Bulletin de l'Institut Français d'Archéologie Orientale* 112:447–464.

Valbelle, D., and C. Rilly. 2012. *Les stèles de l'an 3 d'Aspelta*. Cairo.

Vandersleyen, C. 1995. *L'Egypte et la vallée du Nil. 2. De la fin de l'Ancien Empire à la fin du Nouvel Empire*. Paris.

Vercoutter, J. 1965. "Excavations at Mirgissa II (October 1963–March 1964)." *Kush* 13:62–73.

Welsby, D. 2001. *Life on the Desert Edge: Seven Thousand Years of Settlement in the Northern Dongola Reach, Sudan*. 2 volumes. Oxford.

Wenig, S. 1978. *Africa in Antiquity*, vol. 2, *The Catalogue*. Brooklyn.

Acknowledgments

This book has its origins in three Huggins Lectures delivered at Harvard University in Cambridge, Massachusetts (October 18–20, 2016). After fifty-one years of archaeological exploration in Sudan, it is high time to take stock of the discoveries of the Missions of the Universities of Geneva and Neuchâtel, followed by the Swiss-French-Sudanese Archaeological Mission of Kerma–Dukki Gel. The research conducted during these many years would not have been possible without the collaboration of many institutions and individuals, chief among them the directors of the Antiquities Service and Museums of Sudan, represented today by Abd el-Rahman Ali Mohamed and our eternal friend Salah el-Din Mohamed Ahmed. Dominique Valbelle and, more recently, Séverine Marchi shared in the responsibility of directing the expeditions. Matthieu Honegger and Marc Bundi were ever at my side. The support of the Swiss National Science Foundation and the Swiss Cultural Office deserves special mention, as does the backing of the French Ministry of Foreign Affairs and International Development. Our work was made possible, in large part, by the financial support of UMR 8167, the Orient and Mediterranean Division of the French National Center for Scientific Research, and the University of Paris, Sorbonne.

Our expedition members proved their worth as they intrepidly faced the rigors of the climate during our investigations in the field. First and foremost, I thank Marion Berti, Gérard Deuber, Orianne Dewitte, Alfred Hidber, Thomas Kohler, Juliette Laroye, Séverine Marchi, Inès Matter-Horisberger, Alain Peillex, Françoise Plojoux-Rochat, Pascale Rummler-Kohler, and Jean-Michel Willot. I am also grateful for the contributions of Béatrice Privati and Philippe Ruffieux, who undertook the chronological study of the ceramics. Daniel Berti, Bernard Noël Chagny, Nicolas Faure, Jean-François Gout, Pascale Rummler-Kohler, and Jean-Baptiste Sevette were our photographers. During our last season, Tomasz Herbich and Robert Ryndziewiez conducted, under the auspices of the Polish Institute of Mediterranean Studies of Warsaw, a geomagnetic survey that yielded exceptional results. Just as important as these colleagues are our faithful Sudanese workers of many years, who honed their exceptional skills under the direction of *raïs* Gad Abdallah, Saleh Melieh, Abdel Razek, Omer Nuri, and Idriss Hassan Idriss.

I am equally grateful to Nora Ferrero, Cléa Marcuard, and Pierre Meyrat for their careful reading of the manuscript, and to Larissa Hordynsky for her translation. Color artwork program was made possible with the generous financial support of the W. E. B. DuBois Research Institute. All illustrations are kindly provided by the Swiss-French-Sudanese Archaeological Mission of Kerma-Dukki Gel. I thank you all for your invaluable contributions.

Index

Note: Page citations in *italic* type indicate illustrations.